# CIDER APPLES

National Library of Australia Cataloguing-in-Publication entry

Author: Thornton, C., author.

Title: Cider apples / C. Thornton.

ISBN: 9781925110524 (paperback)

Series: Rare and heritage fruit ; Set 1, no. 2.

Notes: Includes bibliographical references and index.

Subjects: Cider.
Apples--Heirloom varieties.
Apples--Varieties.

Dewey Number: 634.117

ABN 67 099 575 078

PO Box 9113, Brighton, 3186, Victoria, Australia
www.leavesofgoldpress.com

# RARE AND HERITAGE FRUIT CULTIVARS #2

# CIDER APPLES

The Old Quining

C. Thornton

# - RARE AND HERITAGE FRUIT -

## THE SERIES

―――――――――――⌒⌒⌒――――――――――――

### SET #1

## RARE AND HERITAGE FRUIT

# - CULTIVARS -

www.leavesofgoldpress.com

# ABOUT RARE AND HERITAGE FRUIT[1]

This book is one of a series written for 'backyard farmers' of the 21st century. The series focuses on rare and heritage fruit in Australia, although it includes much information of interest to fruit enthusiasts in every country.

For the purpose of this series, rare fruits are species neither indigenous to nor commercially cultivated in any given region.

'Heritage' or 'heirloom' fruits such as old-fashioned varieties[2] of apple, quince, fig, plum, peach and pear are increasingly popular due to their diverse flavours, excellent nutritional qualities and other desirable characteristics.

It is much easier for modern supermarkets to offer only a limited range of fruit cultivars (i.e. varieties) to consumers, instead of dozens of different kinds of apples, pears etc. During the 19th and early 20th centuries, however, the diversity was huge. Old

---

1     *Note: this introduction is identical in every handbook in the Rare and Heritage Fruit series.*

2     *The correct term in this case is 'cultivars'; however most people are more familiar with the term 'varieties' and although it is not strictly accurate, we use the terms interchangeably in this series.*

nursery catalogues were filled with numerous named varieties of fruits, nuts and berries, few of which are available these days.

What are heritage fruits? 'An heirloom plant, heirloom variety, heritage fruit (Australia), or (especially in the UK) heirloom vegetable is an old cultivar that is "still maintained by gardeners and farmers particularly in isolated or ethnic communities".[3]

'These may have been commonly grown during earlier periods in human history, but are not used in modern large-scale agriculture. Many heirloom vegetables have kept their traits through open pollination, while fruit varieties such as apples have been propagated over the centuries through grafts and cuttings.'[4]

Broadly speaking, heritage fruits are historic cultivars; those which have initially been selected or bred by human beings and given officially recognised names, before being propagated by successive generations of growers, retaining their genetic integrity far beyond the normal life-span of an individual plant; those which are not protected by a private plant-breeders' licence, but instead belong to the public at large. They are the legacy of our ancestors; living heirlooms; part of humanity's horticultural, vintage and culinary heritage.

Fruit enthusiasts around the globe are currently reviving our horticultural legacy by renovating old orchards and identifying rare, historic fruit varieties. The goal is to make a much wider range of fruit trees available again to the home gardener.

This series of handbooks aims to help.

---

3       Whealy, K. (1990). "Seed Savers Exchange: preserving our genetic heritage". (Transactions of the Illinois State Horticultural Society 123: 80–84.)
4       Heirloom plant. Wikipedia. Accessed October 2013

STORIES

Like people, every fruit cultivar has a name and a story. Take the Granny Smith apple, for example—the most successful Australian apple, instantly identifiable with its smooth green skin, exported world-wide, and now cultivated in numerous countries.

This famous cultivar began in the 1860s as a tiny seedling that chanced to spring up in a compost heap. An orchardist by the name of Mrs Maria Ann Smith lived with her ailing husband in Eastwood, New South Wales (now a suburb of Sydney). She was in her late sixties, a hard worker and the mother of many children.

One autumn day, as usual, Maria Smith drove her horse-drawn wagon home from the Sydney markets, where she had been selling the fruit from her orchard. The wagon possibly contained a few wooden crates she had purchased after selling her produce, in which to transport the next load of wares. One or two leftover Tasmanian-grown French Crab apples might still have been lying in the crates, somewhat battered and past their prime. Imagine 'Granny' Smith, her grey hair tucked up inside her bonnet, trudging down to the creek from which the household drew its water and dumping their decaying remains on its banks.

There in that damp spot, sinking into compost-rich soil, the apple pips lay throughout the winter months. Come spring, one of them split open and a tiny white rootlet appeared. It swiftly bored downwards, stood up and threw off its black seed-case, revealing two perfect, green cotyledons.

The leaves quickly multiplied as the seedling grew, Maria spied it next time she walked down to the creek, the hems of her long black skirts rustling through the ferns. She nurtured the infant tree until it grew up and bore fruit. When at last she picked the first green-skinned apple and took a bite, she must have been surprised by the crisp, hard flesh and sharp taste. No doubt she used it to make pies and other desserts for her sick husband and numerous grand-children, thus discovering that this new cultivar was good for both cooking and eating.

She shared the apples with friends and neighbours, allowing them to cut scion-wood from her tree and graft their own cloned versions. Locally, word of the apple's qualities spread.

'Smith died only a couple years after her discovery, but dozens of Granny Smith apple trees lived on in her neighbours' orchards. Her new cultivar did not receive widespread attention until, in 1890, it was exhibited as 'Smith's Seedling' at the Castle Hill Agricultural and Horticultural Show. The following year it won the prize for cooking apples under the name 'Granny Smith's Seedling'.

'The apple became a hit. In 1895 the New South Wales Department of Agriculture officially recognized the cultivar and began growing it at the Government Experimental Station in Bathurst, New South Wales, recommending its properties as a late-picking cooking apple for potential export.

'During the first half of the 20th century the government actively promoted the apple, leading to its widespread acceptance. However, its worldwide fame grew from the fact that it was such a good 'keeper'. Because of its excellent shelf life the Granny Smith could be transported over long distances in cold storage and in most seasons. Granny Smiths were exported in enormous quantities after the First World War, and by 1975 forty percent of Australia's apple crop was Granny Smiths. By this time the apple was

being grown extensively elsewhere in the southern
hemisphere, as well as in France, Great Britain and
the United States.'

'The advent of the Granny Smith Apple is now cel-
ebrated annually in Eastwood with the Granny Smith
Festival.[5]

Fruit cultivar stories continue to arise in the 21st
century. From AAP, February 21, 2010, 'Mudgee
Farmer Bruce Davis Creates New Fruit':

> Is it a plum? Is it a peach? It's probably a pleach, as
> it's a morph of the two tasty stone fruits. Whatever it
> is, it's a love child of the two, accidentally created by
> a retired NSW farmer.
>
> Bruce Davis from Mudgee in the state's central west
> couldn't believe it when he discovered he had grown a
> cross between a peach and a plum. The fruit looks like
> a peach from the outside, but resembles a red plum
> when bitten into. The unusual fruit is believed to be
> the first of its kind ever grown in the state.
>
> Mr Davis grows peach and blood plum trees alongside
> each other and believes the peach/plum tree may have
> grown from compost that contained plum seeds.
>
> "It's a really interesting piece of fruit and it's very
> tasty," Mr Davis said.
>
> A cross between a plum and an apricot, known as a
> pluot, has been grown in the past, but a peach and a
> plum is a new combination for NSW, Primary Indus-
> tries Minister Steve Whan said.
>
> Industry and Investment NSW Mudgee horticultur-
> ist Susan Marte said this was the first time she had
> heard of anyone accidentally crossing the two fruits.

---

5      *Granny Smith Festival. Wikipedia. Accessed October*
*2013.*

## NAMES

The origins of the Mudgee pleach and the Granny Smith apple are two of many intriguing fruit stories, but sometimes the name—or names—of cultivars tells yet another story, an etymological one. Names may be inspired by the place a new cultivar was discovered, by the person who selected or bred it, by the shape, flavour, colour or use of the fruit, by an event that took place around the time of discovery, by somebody's sweetheart, or any number of other factors.

Names, too, may be multiplied.

The Granny Smith apple was discovered after the advent of newspapers. If you forgot what the prize-winning cultivar was called, you could look it up and there it would be, in black and white. This was not the case for many ancient cultivars.

The Granny Smith apple's probable mother, the French Crab, itself boasts twenty-six listed synonyms, probably invented by forgetful apple-growers.

Another instance of numerous synonyms is the French cider apple whose name is Calville Rouge D'Hiver, meaning 'Calville Winter Red'. It arose in the late 1500s, and as its popularity spread across Europe, the first thing that happened was that people translated the name into their own language: 'Teli Piros Kalvil', 'Roter Winter Calville', 'Calvilla Rossa di Pasqua', 'Cerveny Zimni Hranac' etc.

Next, when absent-minded peasants could not remember the name of this excellent red fruit, they gave it another one. Imagine a weather-beaten farmer in some isolated French village scratching his beard and musing, 'It was something to do with "Calville". "Calville Rouge," perchance?' Across the valley in another village, a cider-brewer was knitting his (or her) puzzled brow and saying, 'It was something to do with winter, I am thinking, or was it autumn? "Pomme d'Automne"?' Further afield, a third Frenchman shrugged his shoulders and declared, 'Devil take me if I can remember how it is called, but it is big and red like the heart of a bull, so let us name it "Coeur de Boeuf."'

Fanciful, perhaps, but this might explain why, on the database of the UK's National Fruit Collection, there are more than a hundred synonyms listed for Calville Rouge D'Hiver.

Words are forever evolving. Even when cultivar names stay the same, the language around them is changing and their original meaning becomes lost in the mists of time.

One example of this is the grape cultivar Cabernet Sauvignon, which is considered a relatively new variety, being the product of a chance 17th century crossing between Cabernet franc and Sauvignon blanc.

'Cabernet franc' can be etymologically traced back to 'French Black Grape' (from the Latin word 'caput' which means 'black vine'). The word 'Sauvignon' is believed to be derived from the French 'sauvage', meaning 'wild' and to refer to the grape being a wild grapevine native to France. 'Blanc,' of course, means 'white'. 'Cabernet Sauvignon' no longer means 'Wild Black Grape' in modern French—that would translate as something like 'Vigne Noir Sauvage'. The ancient cultivar name has now taken on its own meaning and is virtually synonymous with the wine made from it.

It is interesting to compare typical cider apple names with, say, typical peach or perry pear names. French words abound among heritage cider apple cultivars, reflecting their roots in medieval Normandy. To the ears of English-speakers these names may sound rather mysterious and aristocratic, until you translate them: for example, Gros Bois, Jaune de Vitré, Moulin à Vent du Calvados, Noël des Champs, Belle Fille de la Manche, Petite Sorte du Parc Dufour and Groin D'âne translate respectively as Big Wood, Yellow Glass, Windmill of Calvados, Christmas Field, Beautiful Girl of the English Channel, Small Kind of Park of the Oven and Donkey's Groin.

Some names of heritage perry pears give us an insight into the bawdy, rustic humour of the perry-drinking English peasants who originally selected them; Ram's Cods, Startle Cock and Bloody Bastard to mention a few.

Heritage grape cultivars have names that come from all over Europe, particularly France and Italy.

Figs go back even further. Humans were cultivating them around 9400 BC, a thousand years before wheat and rye were domesticated. Their names, in English at least, are often drawn from their colour and their place of origin—Brown Turkey, White Adriatic, Black Genoa, Pink Jerusalem, Green Ischia ...

Peaches, a more 'modern' fruit in terms of their popularity and breeding, often bear invented names with fancy spellings, such as Florda Glo, Earligrande, Harbrite and Dixigem.

## 'IMMORTAL' DNA

Another major difference between stone fruit and fruits such as grapes, figs and apples is their ability to grow 'true' to their parents from seed. Stone fruits are far more homozygous than their ancient cousins the pomes (apples, pears etc.) and the grapes. Growers do graft them, but if you plant their seeds the new tree will bear fruit that's fairly similar to that of the parent tree. This means that the centuries-old grafting traditions, the fierce cherishing, the careful bequeathing and the meticulous labelling that accompany pome fruits, grapes and other heterozygotes are not seen as often in the world of peaches and nectarines. This is why many of their cultivar names seem so different, arising as they do from highly organised commercial breeding programmes of the 20th and 21st centuries.

Unlike the seedlings of say, peaches and nectarines, seedling apples are an example of 'extreme heterozygotes', in that rather than inheriting DNA from their parents to create a new apple with those characteristics, they are instead significantly different from their parents.'[6] (Humans are rather like apples in that way, though not as extreme.)

Returning to our green-skinned Australian apple— 'Because the Granny Smith is a chance (and rare) mutation, its seeds tend to produce trees whose fruit have a much less appealing taste. To preserve the exact genetic code of any plant variety, a stick of the wood has to be 'cloned'. It has to be grafted onto new roots (or planted directly into the ground, but this is uncommon for trees). Thus, all the Granny Smith apple trees grown today are cuttings of cuttings of cuttings from the original Smith tree in Sydney.'[7]

Cloning by grafting means that the heritage trees— and shrubs—which have survived through the years

6    John Lloyd and John Mitchinson (2006). QI: The Complete First Series – QI Factoids
7    Stirzaker, Richard (2010). Out of the Scientist's Garden: A Story of Water and Food. Collingwood, VIC: CSIRO Pub.

are genetically identical to their ancestors. Indeed, the heritage plants of today possess exactly the same genetic code as the original trees that arose centuries ago in Asia and Europe. For example, another heritage apple cultivar, 'Court Pendu Plat', is thought to be 1500 years old—the oldest one in existence. Introduced into Europe during Roman times, the living wood from that same tree flourishes to this day, right here in the Great Southern Land.

## RARE AND HERITAGE FRUIT IN AUSTRALIA

Many of the rare and heritage fruits that exist in Australia today are clonally descended from plants brought to our shores by the early European settlers, when few, if any, quarantine laws existed. Good luck rather than good stock monitoring limited the number of plant diseases unintentionally imported during the early days of colonization. Fortunately, by 1879 it was recognised that in order to prevent the introduction of serious pests and diseases, quarantine measures were needed. In 1908, the Commonwealth Quarantine service came into operation and took over local quarantine stations in every Australian state.

However, before 1879, there was no limit to the varieties of fruiting plants that could be imported into this country. Many of those old genetic lines survive to this day but sadly, many others have been lost.

Fortunately, Australia is one of only two countries free of fire blight, a serious and ineradicable disease that wiped out millions of apple, pear, loquat and quince trees in Europe and the USA during the 1900s. This means that when certain heritage cultivars went extinct elsewhere, they remained safe in this country.

Some have now been restored to their region of origin, now grafted onto fire blight-resistant rootstock.

Over the course of the decades since 1879 Australian fruit growers imported (through quarantine) the latest new cultivars bred by overseas agricultural research stations. Year by year, as scientific advances in breeding and genetics were made, the older cultivars fell out of fashion and were swept aside in favour of the new. They, too, became part of our almost forgotten fruit inheritance.

## COMMERCIAL CULTIVARS

Naturally, plant breeders strive to provide the products demanded by the market. Commercial orchardists want to purchase heavy-bearing trees with high disease resistance, whose fruit ripens all at the same time to save on picking costs. Wholesalers want fruit that keeps in storage for a long time without spoiling, and can be shipped without damage. Only firm-fleshed, bruise-resistant fruit will survive modern-day processing. After harvesting, apples, for instance, are tipped into crates, then passed along a conveyor belt through machinery that washes and brushes them clean of insecticides and dirt. This process removes some of the fruit's natural protective coating, so the machines re-apply a commercial grade wax before polishing them to a high shine and pasting a plastic label onto each one. Then the apples are packed into cartons for shipping to markets and stores.

Supermarket shoppers demand visually attractive fruit—large, regular in shape, unblemished and with highly coloured skin. Consumers also choose fruit with extra sugar content and juiciness.

All these characteristics, nonetheless, do not necessarily give rise to the best flavour or nutrition. To pick a tree-ripened fruit from your own back yard and bite into it is to experience the taste of fresh food as our forefathers knew it. Growing and preserving their own food, unconcerned with transportability and long storage times, they aimed for a wide variety of fruits, each of which had a unique and delicious taste.

Rare fruit, heritage and heirloom fruit enthusiasts across the world are reviving our horticultural legacy by renovating old orchards and sourcing 'lost' historic and unusual fruit varieties. Their goal is to encourage community participation and to make a wide range of fruit trees available again to the home gardener.

This series of handbooks aims to help.

## WHY PRESERVE RARE AND HERITAGE FRUITS?

• They provide access to a wider range of unique and delicious flavours.
• We can enjoy the nutritional benefits of fresh, tree-ripened food.
• Biodiversity: The preservation of a wide range of vital genetic material helps to insure against the ravages of pests and diseases in the future.
• They allow a longer harvesting season, with early and late ripening.
• Culture: heritage varieties, with their interesting assortment of names, are living history.

**Collections of heritage fruit trees are precious. Anyone who is the custodian of an old tree should treasure it.**

# CONTENTS

With thanks to

Claude Jolicoeur, author of 'The New Cider Maker's Handbook',

David Pickering, Technical Officer, Science and Research, NSW Dept. of Primary Industries, Orange, New South Wales,

Jez Howat of 146 Cider Company, author of the article 'Styling Cider' in collaboration with Andrew Lea of Wittenham Hill Cider,

Australian orchardist Peter Cooke for devising his Flowering Group system, sharing his meticulously recorded flowering data and providing other information,

The Cider Workshop members
www.ciderworkshop.com

# ABOUT CIDER APPLES

This handbook is about choosing cider apple cultivars. For instructions on how to make cider (and perry) at home, see our other handbooks in this series.

The cultivars listed in this book were all available for purchase in Australia at the time of publication.

Cider apples are apple cultivars grown for their use in cider production. Cider is an alcoholic beverage obtained from the fermentation of the juice of apples. Any apples can be used to make cider, but for a good result it is important that the fruit contains high sugar levels, which encourage fermentation and raise the final alcohol levels. Cider apples therefore often have higher sugar levels than dessert (eating) and culinary (cooking) apples.[1]

The difference between cider apples and dessert or culinary apples can be likened to the difference between wine grapes and table grapes.

That said, a few cultivars that are not specifically 'cider apples' have been included here, because traditionally they are valued for their use in cider-making. Golden Hornet, renowned for its ornamental value, is

---

1    'Cider apple'. Wikipedia, accessed October 2013

an excellent apple for cider, and Bramley's Seedling, famous for its culinary uses, is another.

In the UK there are two distinct cider-making styles: Eastern Counties style, using dessert and culinary apples, and West Country style, using only recognised cider apples.

### FLAVOUR TYPES

In the United Kingdom in 1903, the Long Ashton Agricultural Research Station categorised cider apples into four main types according to the nature of their flavour components:

**Sweets** This group is low in tannins (<0.2%) and acidity (<0.45%).

'Sweet varieties are the blandest of the four categories, being low in both components. They are useful to blend with ciders from the more strongly flavoured varieties, which, by themselves, would be too extreme in taste and aroma to be palatable.'[2]

**Sharps** This group is high in acidity (>0.45%) and low in tannins (<0.2%). The high acidity, together with that from the bittersharp group, can add a desirable 'bite' to the cider.

'Sharp varieties, so called because the predominant characteristic is that of acidity, are encountered less frequently today, possibly because culinary fruit, which has a similar flavour balance, can be substituted for this class. There are, however, recognised full sharp cider varieties, including Brown's Apple.'[3]

The natural acids in cider apples include malic, citric, lactic and acetic acids.

**Bittersweets** This group is low in acidity (<0.45%) and high in tannin (>0.2%).

---

2      *Cider Apples'. NACM Cider Makers LTD., UK*
3      *ibid*

'Bittersweet apples impart the characteristic flavour of English ciders; as the name implies they are low in acid and high in tannin. The latter is responsible for two sensations on the palate—astringency and bitterness. In the bittersweet apple, there is a whole range of combinations of these two characteristics, varying from little astringency coupled with intense bitterness to very marked astringency coupled with mild bitterness.'[4]

In particular, a certain amount of bitterness is expected in ciders of the West Country Style.

**Bittersharps** This group is high in both acidity (>0.45%) and tannin (>0.2%).[5]

'These are fairly high in acid and tannin, although the latter component does not show the wide range of flavours exhibited by the bittersweet. Stoke Red is a good example.'[6]

It is the sweet apples that provide the majority of the alcoholic 'base' for the cider, while apples from the other three categories provide the characteristic tastes, texture and complexity found in a good cider.[7]

Acid and tannin levels are always affected by the tree's locality, seasonal conditions, irrigation, age etc. so it is only possible to give estimates for each cultivar.

The English grouping of cider apple varieties has been in place for a long time. Classification varies slightly in France, where they have a six category system. The French categories are shown here with the approximate translation:

4     *ibid*
5     *Cider apple. Wikipedia, accessed October 2013*
6     *'Cider Apples'. NACM Cider Makers LTD., UK*
7     *'Cider Apples' Okanagan Plant Improvement Corporation.*

*Amere*: bitter
*Douce amere*: bittersweet
*Douce*: sweet
*Acidulee*: acidic
*Aigre amere*: bittersharp
*Aigre*: sour, tart, sharp

Both the English and the French system of categories are based on the acid and tannin content of the apple juice.

### SINGLE VARIETY CIDERS

Novices to cider-making sometimes assume that they can plant a cider-apple tree in the garden and make cider from the fruit every year. In theory this is possible, but not if you want a consistently drinkable beverage! The secret of delicious cider is blending to creat a balanced flavour, and for that you need juice from several different flavour-type apple cultivars.

To make the best cider, apples must be chosen from each category. The theory is that a well balanced cider is made up of 30% bitter apples, 30% bittersweet apples, 30% sweet apples and 10% tart. However ciders produced by the same varieties can sometimes be very different from each other. The cider-maker's art is to achieve the optimum blends, finding the right proportions which result in a high quality, unique cider.

There are very few cultivars that may make a good cider all by themselves, with no need for any additives; Kingston Black has been known to make an excellent single variety (SV) cider. Traditionally, Stoke Red and possibly Improved Foxwhelp have also been used for this purpose. Such apples are prized in both single variety and multi-variety blends of cider.

However, these are exceptions, and even *they* do not always produce high quality SV cider, because the quality of cider apples—as with every fruit—varies seasonally, according to annual fluctuations in the weather and other growing conditions. One year might produce an excellent vintage while the following year produces an average or poor one. Of course, you could blend different vintages of the same apple to achieve a good SV cider, but why bother to wait for next year's crop when you could easily make a great brew with a wide selection from this year's harvest?

Note: An apple's flavour is influenced by factors such as local climate, the soil, the tree's proximity to the coast and its altitude. All these variables and others come into play. The same apple cultivar can develop subtly different flavour characteristics depending on which part of the country it grows in.

The following apples have all been offered commercially as single variety ciders, with varying results: Kingston Black, Eggleton Styre, Court Royal, Somerset Redstreak, Northern Spy, Sweet Alford, Sweet Coppin, Stoke Red, Tremlett's Bitter, Winesap, Dabinett. and Beauty of Bath.

'Within the last couple of decades, cider makers have been marketing "single variety" ciders, following the fashion for named grapes in wines.

'Apples are not like grapes, so apples with all the features to make a well balanced cider are few. Blends of apples for cider were the norm, and generally still are. If a good apple variety is available, its features will add to the quality of the cider. Removing that variety will deduct from the quality of the blend.

'The commercial single variety ciders are often not truly single variety at all – they will usually be considerably less than 100% juice, and will have had acid and sweeteners added to achieve a balanced and palatable flavour. Sadly, as with many commercial things, the idea of selling a single variety cider is a fashionable concept but one not bedded in any historical substance or justification.'[8]

When growing apples to make your own cider you'll want to choose cultivars whose flavour characteristics complement each other. To help you in this decision, a table is included at the back of this book. It lists cider apples by their flavour types, flowering groups and harvest times, so that you can select trees which pollinate each other and estimate the storage times needed for earlier-ripening fruit.

### CIDER AROUND THE WORLD

The UK, France and the USA are the main sources of heritage cider apples. In France, where they have been drinking it since at least the year 1130, the alcoholic drink made from apples is called 'cidre'. In the US and Canada, it is called 'hard cider'. (They use the terms 'cider', 'sweet cider' or 'soft cider' to denote non-alcoholic apple juice.)

The most obvious difference between British and American cider styles is sweetness. The Brits prefer a much 'drier' taste than the Americans, and to that end they cultivated numerous cider apples with that attribute. The United Kingdom has the highest per capita consumption of cider, as well as the largest cider-producing companies in the world.[9]

---

8      *'Styling Cider' by Jez Howat and Andrew Lea. Source: Cider Workshop www.ciderworkshop.com*
9      *ibid*

Some English heritage cider apple cultivars that are grown in Australia are 'Kingston Black', 'Stoke Red' and 'Bulmer's Norman'. 'Kingston Black' is probably named after the village of Kingston, near Taunton, Somerset; 'Stoke Red' is from Rodney Stoke, between Cheddar and Wells. Australia also has 'Breakwell's Seedling', from Wales.

French *pommes à cidre* in Australia include the sweet flavour-type 'Bedan' and the tart 'French Crab'. American heritage cider apples cultivated in Australia include 'Baldwin' and 'Yates'.

### POLLINATION

Most apple cultivars need to be pollinated by others, in order to produce fruit.

**Self-fertile** apple cultivars (also known as self-compatible or self-pollinating) can produce fruit without needing to be pollinated by another apple tree, although pollen from a nearby apple cultivar will cause *more* fruit to set.

Trees that cannot fertilize themselves are called **self-sterile**, which means they need cross pollination for the production of fruit.

'**Ploidy**' is defined as 'the number of sets of chromosomes in a cell, or in the cells of an organism.' Why do we need to know a bit about it? So that we know which apple cultivars can pollinate each other.

**Diploid:** Most apple cultivars are diploid (containing two complete sets of chromosomes, one from each parent.) They give pollen to other trees blossoming at the same time, and take some in exchange.

**Triploid and tetraploid:** Some, however, are triploid, with three sets of chromosomes instead of two or even tetraploid, with four!

The pollen of these apple cultivars will not pollinate other apple trees. They are 'pollen takers' not 'pollen givers'. Generally they are not self-fertile, and therefore need another compatible apple variety nearby to pollinate them. (Some triploid varieties, nonetheless, have a degree of partial self-fertility).

In short, if you are planting a triploid cultivar, you should to make sure there is a nearby 'companion' apple tree that blossoms at the same time.

And if you want the *companion* tree to set fruit, you must either choose a self-fertile apple variety, or plant a third tree. The third tree must be either a crabapple, or another apple cultivar that blooms at the same time as the companion, so that the companion can exchange pollen with it. The third tree can also donate some pollen to the triploid.

'Although the pollination requirements might be inconvenient, triploid varieties have several advantages which make them desirable for the home or community orchard: they usually produce vigorous trees, which can support large crops, the apples are often quite large, they usually display a good degree of natural disease resistance and they can often survive in difficult conditions.'[10]

### 'POLLINATION GROUPS' OR 'FLOWERING GROUPS'

These are groups of different cultivars that flower around the same time, thus providing pollen for each other.

In the suburbs, at least, gardeners really don't have to worry much about apple pollinators because bees

---

10      *'Triploid Apple Varieties'. www.orangepippin.com,* accessed October 2013

can fly more than 6.5 km (four miles) to gather food. Odds are that some neighbouring garden within that radius will have an apple tree flowering at the right time. (And many insects other than bees accomplish pollination in any case.)

However if your apple trees are failing to set fruit, consider planting a polleniser.

An individual apple tree usually blossoms for about seven days, during which the buds open and the flowers expand into full bloom before finally dropping their petals.

By studying the flowering habits of trees, researchers have identified the dates when particular cultivars are normally at full bloom. This is the optimum time for them to be pollinated. The best pollination partners for your tree are cultivars that bloom within a six-day overlap period.

Horticulturists divide cultivars into convenient flowering groups. The reason groups are used, instead of dates, is because variations in local climate (such as altitude, latitude and proximity to the coast), in addition to variations in annual weather patterns, cause trees to flower on different dates each year. Trees have no respect for calendars!

By grouping cultivars we know that trees in Group 1, for example, are pollinated by groups 1 and 2, while trees in Group 2 are pollinated by groups 1, 2 and 3. Thus we can work out which trees to plant near each other as pollinators.

The only problem is that horticultural organisations across the world use their own individual Flowering Group systems. There is no consistency, and there appears to be no single global standard. Some use alphabetical letters as labels, some use numerals;

some call them 'Pollination Groups' and others call them 'Flowering Groups'. There might be anything from two to nine groups in a system.

In the UK, 'Trees Online', for example, has groups coded from C1 to C5 while Ashridge Trees boasts eight groups from A to H and the Royal Horticultural Society divides apples into seven Flowering Groups, 1 to 7. In Australia, Woodbridge Fruit Trees groups apple cultivars into 'Early, Middle, Late and Extra Late flowering', while JFT Nurseries simplify everything by dividing apples into just two groups, 1 and 2.

France has four official apple flowering seasons.

1st: cultivars flowering before April 25;

2nd: cultivars in bloom from April 25 to May 10;

3rd: cultivars flowering between 10 and 25 May;

4th: cultivars blooming after May 25

In southern Australia where apples thrive, even the coldest winters are mild by UK and French standards, so apart from the fact that the seasons are opposite, Australian flowering times are also relatively earlier.

They are spread over a longer period, too. In Melbourne, the apples 'Dorset Golden' (low chill) and 'Anna' flower in the first week of August. 'Court Pendu Plat' is the last to blossom, in December. This means that apples as a species are in bloom for five months!

To add to the confusion, Australian orchardist Peter Cooke of MiApple Heritage Apple Trees in Victoria, has noticed that 'apple trees seem to have hormones!'

'If two trees with different flowering times are growing close together,' he wrote in 2013, 'they often flower together. I notice this particularly in my potted tree nursery. I have Stokes Red (usually week 7) growing beside Vérité (week 6)—they both flowered together in week 9 last season.'

In this handbook we are using flowering data based on the system devised by Peter Cooke, who writes, 'My seasons are too irregular from year to year so I don't record flowering dates. My orchard flowering times are all in weeks (Sundays) relative to when Jonathan is in full flower in week 3 (on a Sunday).

'If a variety has full flowers over a period of three (Sunday) weeks I will record it as for example 4—6 meaning it had full flowers in weeks 4, 5 and 6 relative to Jonathan which flowered fully in week 3. Anna usually flowers four or five weeks before Jonathan so I record it as minus 2.'

It sounds confusing but it's not. If you don't live in the suburbs near other apple trees, all you have to do is find out which Flowering Group your chosen cultivar belongs to. It will be pollinated by all other cultivars in that group as well as those in the groups on either side of it.

In cases where we have no Australian flowering data we have used the best information to hand, whether it be from the Royal Horticultural Society (RHS), the French Ministry of Agriculture or elsewhere.

Note: Crabapples make good pollinators in apple orchards, because they generally flower profusely and over a long period. Growers with orchards of single varieties sometimes provide bouquets of crabapple blossoms in drums or pails in the orchard for pollenisers. You can also make cider and jelly out of crabapples.

## HARVEST TIMES

Apples vary greatly in their ripening and harvesting times. In southern Australia, for example, early-ripening cider apples such as Breakwell's Seedling and Improved Foxwhelp are ready in February. Michelin, Somerset Redstreak, Bulmer's Norman and Sweet Coppin can be picked in March; Dabinett, Kingston Black, Clozette, Stokes Red and Yarlington Mill are April apples and King David and Brown Snout ripen in April/May, while Calville Blanc D'Hiver is harvested as late as June.

Again, it has been difficult to find Australian apple-ripening data, but we have provided the best information available to us from various sources.

### Maturité de Brassage

In France, orchardists divide cider apples into *maturité de brassage*, or 'brewing-ripeness' seasons:

1st season: The group of cultivars whose fruits reach brewing-ripeness before 10th October.

2nd season: The group of cultivars whose fruits reach brewing-ripeness before between 10th October and 30th November.

3rd season: The group of cultivars whose fruits reach brewing-ripeness after 1st December.[11]

### THE BULMERS

H.P. Bulmer is a cider-making company which began in 1887 in Hereford, England. The founder was Henry Percival (Percy) Bulmer, the twenty-year-old son

---

11     *Variétés recommandées de pommiers à cidre, pour les départements de Normandie, de Bretagne, et du Maine et Perche / par Ministère de l'agriculture. 1960*

of the local rector at Credenhill, the Reverend Charles H. Bulmer and his wife Mary. He is said to have taken his mother's advice to make a career in food or drink, "because neither ever go out of fashion".[12]

By 2013, HP Bulmer was manufacturing 65% of the five hundred million litres of cider sold annually in the United Kingdom and the bulk of the UK's cider exports.[13]

The Bulmers did not only brew cider—they imported French cider apple cultivars ('Bulmer's Norman' apple bears the family name) and bred new ones such as 'Improved Foxwhelp'. They had a huge influence on the proliferation of cider apples in the United Kingdom.

### CHILLING REQUIREMENTS

Most cider varieties have high chill requirements to break winter dormancy, as they originated from the cooler climates of Northern Europe. Kingston Black and Stoke Red have very high chilling requirements, and both may have problems in breaking dormancy in all but the coldest apple growing districts in Australia, such as Orange and Batlow in New South Wales, or the cooler southern states of Victoria and Tasmania[14].

### KEEPING QUALITIES

If cider-makers depend on using cultivars that ripen at different times, they have to make their cider in batches. This can be time-consuming and costly. In order to narrow production down to one or two batches—for example one in the middle of harvest

12    "Bulmers – How It All Began". Herefordshire County Council. Accessed 29 September 2007.
13    'Bulmers' Wikipedia, accessed October 2013
14    David Pickering.

season and one towards the end—cider-makers have to store their earlier-ripening apples.

'Almost any kind of apple will keep for three or four months, or even longer, if stored properly. It's cheap and easy to do. All you need is newspaper to layer between the fruit, well-ventilated boxes, baskets, sacks or netting to contain them in, and a cool, dry, dark, airy shed or cellar to house them.

'The main causes of apple spoilage are time, bruises, and contact with a rotten spot on another apple.'[15]

Nonetheless, the length of time apples can be preserved in storage depends more on variety and harvest time than simply storing them well.

Storage duration can be increased by selecting long-keeping varieties of apples. Tart and thick-skinned apples generally keep longer than sweet or thin-skinned ones. Good 'keepers' also have very firm flesh.

### DEFINITIONS

**Acidity**: Various natural fruit acids are an important component in both cidermaking and the finished beverage. They are present in both apples and cider, having direct influences on the colour, balance and taste of the cider.

**Biennial bearing** is a problem in some fruit trees, particularly apples and pears, where they crop heavily in one year and then produce little or nothing the next. Some cultivars are naturally biennial but

---

15    *'Here are some simple tips on how to store apples for a long, long time.' Don Fallick. www.backwoodshome.com Issue #41 September/October, 1996*

weather conditions and soil fertility can contribute to the problem.[16]

**Brix:** Degrees Brix is the sugar content of an aqueous solution, traditionally used in the wine, cider, perry, sugar, fruit juice, and honey industries. One degree Brix is 1 gram of sucrose in 100 grams of solution.[17]

**Codlin** is the old English term for immature apples, hence 'codlin' or 'codling' moths, whose larvae attack young fruits.[18]

**Cross-pollination** occurs when pollen is delivered to a flower from a flower on a different plant.

**Cultivar:** A cultivar is a plant or group of plants that have been created or selected by humans and maintained through cultivation. Plant varieties, by contrast, are those which may have arisen naturally, moulded and selected by the forces of nature.

**pH:** Strength of acidity is measured according to pH, with most grape wines, for example, having a pH between 2.9 and 3.9. Generally, the lower the pH, the higher the acidity in the wine. However, there is no direct connection between total acidity and pH. It is possible to find fruit liquors with a high pH and high acidity.[19]

**Pippin:** an apple tree that has grown from a pip, or seed.

---

16      *'Fruit: biennial bearing' The Royal Horticultural Society. Accessed October 2013.*

17      *Brix. Wikipedia Accessed October 2013*

18      *Apples Old and New, by Clive Winmill Edition, 5. Publisher, Badger's Keep, 1997*

19      *Bellman, R. B.; Gallander, J. F. (1979). "Wine Deacidification". In Chichester, C. O.; Mrak, Emil Marcel; Stewart, George Franklin. Advances in Food Research Vol. 25. Academic Press.*

**Rootstock**: In grafting, this term refers to a plant, sometimes just a stump, which already has an established, healthy root system, onto which a cutting or a bud from another plant is grafted.[20]

**Russet**: Russeting on apples is a particular type of skin, slightly rough, usually with a greenish-brown to yellowish-brown colour. Many apple cultivars have some natural russeting, but some are almost entirely covered in it, notably the Egremont Russet. Russet apples often exhibit a scent and flavour reminiscent of nuts, and are often very sweet. Despite this, modern apple breeders rarely accept russeting in new apple cultivars (due to it being perceived as unattractive).

An article in the Tasmanian newspaper 'The Examiner' on 24 January 1903, headed 'How to Make Good Cider', states: 'The russet is one of the best of apples for this purpose...'

Russet apples also go under the name "rusticoat", "russeting" and "leathercoat". The last name was known in Shakespeare's time.[21]

**Spur bearing**: Most apples produce fruit buds on wood that's at least two years old. These fruit buds are called 'spurs', and their stems are usually short, stubby and wrinkled. Most apple cultivars belong to the spur bearing group.

**Tip-bearing**: True tip bearers produce fruit buds at the tip of slender shoots that grew the preceding year. Some apple trees are partial tip-bearers—i.e. their fruit appears on both tips and spurs.

### ETYMOLOGY

---

20    'Rootstock'. Wikipedia Accessed October 2013
21    ibid

The word 'cider' evolved from the Hebrew 'shekhar', a word used for any strong drink. The ancient Romans, who spoke Latin, pronounced 'shekhar' as 'sicera'. In turn this word became 'cisdre', then 'cire', or 'cidre' in Old French. The term 'cidre' meaning 'fermented apple juice' was first recorded circa 1130—1140. By the late 13th century the English word 'cider' had sprung into being. Its meaning gradually narrowed to mean exclusively 'fermented drink made from apples'.

## APPLE PARTS

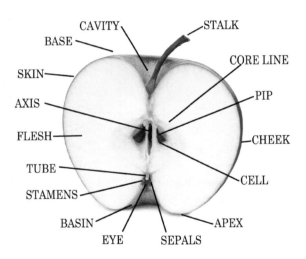

# RARE AND HERITAGE CIDER APPLE CULTIVARS

## IN AUSTRALIA

## A TO C

The Old Quining

## ANTOINETTE

Synonyms: Muscadet de seine-less, Small Muscadet

Provenance: Originated in Rouen, France

Flavour type: Sweet. Recommended by the French Committee of Fruit Cider. Gives a good, dry cider.

Tannin: 2.70 g

Acidity: 1.89 g

Fruit description: Fruit is round and medium to large. Flesh is white, firm, sweet and well-flavoured; the skin is striped with red on green and there is little or no russetting.

Blossom time: Flowers early.

Flowering Group 2.

Harvest time: Ripens mid-season

Ploidy: Diploid

Chilling requirements: Normal chill

Other information: A medium to heavy bearer. Sensitive in wet years to scab, very susceptible to powdery mildew.

*Malus pumila 'Antoinette'. Image: NSW Department of Primary Industries*

## BALDWIN

Synonyms: Woodpecker

Provenance: A chance seedling discovered in Massa-
    chusetts, USA, 1740.

Flavour type: Sharp. A good cider base.

Tannin: 0.059 %, Acid: 0.74 %, Brix:15.3

Fruit description: Medium to large, yellow base flushed
    with orange and striped red. Juicy with sweet to
    sub-acid flavor, aromatic and firm.

Blossom time: Flowering period: Mid—late season

Flowering group: 2

Harvest time: Late in the ripening season

Ploidy: Triploid. Pollination requires two fertile
    varieties in the same flowering group to be within
    bee-range.

Chilling requirements: Normal chill

Other information: Usually a productive and vigorous
    tree. Often a biennial bearer. 'A very popular old
    American apple variety, widely grown for culinary
    use, and a good keeper.'[1]

*Malus pumila 'Baldwin'. Image: The Heritage Fruits Society, Australia*

---

1       *'Baldwin'. www.orangepippin.com Accessed October 2013.*

## BEDAN DES PARTS

Synonyms: Bedon des partes, Bedan des partes.
Note: Bedon or Bédange is a distinct and different variety.

Provenance: Calvados, France. A popular old variety from the 19th century.

Flavour type: Bittersweet. (*Douce amere*). Makes a mild and fragrant apple cider, often mixed with tart and bitter cider apple varieties.

Tannin: 0.172 %

Brix: 11.4

Acid: 0.20 %

pH: 4.26

Fruit description: Sweet, white flesh, small to medium oval or globular, yellow with red haze, no stripes or russetting.

Blossom time: Late blooming.

Flowering group: 4 (French 'Third Season')

Ploidy: Diploid.

Harvest time: Mid to very late season maturity. In France, the 'third season', late November to December.

Chilling requirements: Normal chill

Other information: The tree is precocious and productive. Disease-tolerant, including fire blight.

## BELLE CAUCHOISE

Synonyms: Belle casheuse, Belle cacheuse.

Provenance: France. The name translates as 'Beautiful Cauchoise'. The *Cauchoise* region, or *Pays de Caux*, is one of the last strongholds of the Norman language in Normandy, which itself is a significant cider-producing region

Flavour type: Sweet

Fruit description: Sweet flesh. Small to medium globular or oval, yellow or pale yellow with red haze or red stripes.

Blossom time: flowers early

Flowering group 3—4

Ploidy: Diploid.

Harvest time: ripens mid-season

Chilling requirements: Normal

Other information: Also used for cooking.

*Malus pumila 'Belle Cauchoise'. Image: NSW Department of Primary Industries*

# BLANCHET

Synonyms: Blanc-doux, Blanc, Doux de la lande, Gros-blanc, Blanche. Not to be confused with Blanchette.
Provenance: France
Flavour type: Sharp. Makes excellent cider.
Low tannin, high acid.
Fruit description: Small to medium globular to flat, no stripes, yellow with slight blush, no russetting. This apple is named for the pure white colour of its flesh. The flesh is tender and pleasantly acidic.
Blossom time: Midseason
Flowering group 4—5
Ploidy: Diploid.
Harvest time: 'First season' in France—i.e. an early ripener.
Chilling requirements: Normal chill

# BRAMLEY'S SEEDLING

Synonyms: none known
Provenance: Propagated from a notable seedling; circa 1809—1813 in Nottinghamshire, England
Flavour type: Sharp. Produces a cider with high acid levels which lends to a sharper finish. Has a strong apple flavour with good aromatics. The cider is full bodied with a clean fresh finish.[2]
Acid: 0.85 %
Tannin: 0.08 %
Fruit description: Fruit large, greenish-yellow with broad broken brown and red stripes. Flesh firm, juicy and sharply acid, high in vitamin C.
Blossom time: Mid-late season

---

2    'Seven Oaks Farmhouse Bramleys Seedling Cider'. Mornington Peninsula Wine Centre, Australia

Flowering group: 2

Harvest time: Mid—late season

Ploidy: Triploid. Pollination requires at least one fertile variety in the same flowering group to be within bee-range.

Chilling requirements: Normal

Other information: The standard culinary apple of England. Also used for cider blends. Tree characteristics: scab and mildew resistant. Tree is large, vigorous and spreading, tolerates some shade. Heavy and regular bearer. Vigorous and productive. High vitamin C. (16.0mg/100mg) Considerable tolerance to scab and powdery mildew.

*Malus pumila 'Bramley's Seedling'.*
*Image: The Heritage Fruits Society, Australia*

## BREAKWELL'S SEEDLING

Synonyms: Breakwell Seedling
Provenance: From Perthyre, Monmouth, Wales. Propagated by George Breakwell.
Flavour type: Bittersharp; produces a thin, light, average cider.
Tannin: 0.23 %
Acidity: 0.64 %
Fruit description: Medium or small fruit, flat conical, often irregular. Skin smooth waxy, yellow or yellowish-green base colour with dark red stripes or flecked blush over two-thirds of the surface. Flesh white, occasionally reddish, soft, easily bruised, slightly astringent, crisp juicy.
Blossom time: Mid-season bloom;
Flowering group 5
Ploidy: Diploid.
Harvest time: February (early) Good yield, should be harvested promptly as it quickly breaks down and rots.
Chilling requirements: Normal chill
Self-Fertile, produces viable pollen
Other information: Medium, semi-spreading tree with dark luxuriant foliage which is scab-resistant. Heavy cropper.

## BROWN SNOUT

Synonyms: none known
Provenance: Probably from Mr Dent, mid 1800s, Yarkhill, Hereford, England.
Flavour type: bittersweet. The Brown Snout is very popular in traditional cider making. This apple oxidizes very quickly, resulting in a good, rich

colour for the cider. Makes an average mild to medium cider.

Tannin: 0.24 % relatively high tannins

Acidity: 0.24 % relatively low levels of malic acid.

Fruit description: The fruit are small—around 4.5cm in diameter (1-3/4")—and greenish yellow, with patches of russeting, and a large patch of russeting at the calyx end, giving the variety its name.[3]

Blossom time: Late-blooming

Flowering group 5

Harvest time: Late

Pollination: Supposedly self-fertile. Produces more fruit with a pollinator, and produces viable pollen to fertilise other apple trees.

Chilling requirements: Normal chill

Other information: relatively short storage life. Scab susceptible. Very susceptible to fire blight. High yielding.

*Malus pumila 'Brown Snout'*
*Image: Timeout Chicago, Greg Hall's Cider Adventure.*

---

3     'Brown Snout'. *Wikipedia Accessed October 2013.*

## BROWN'S APPLE

Synonyms: none known
Provenance: From South Devon, England.
Flavour type: Sharp; used as a special-purpose cider.
Tannin: 0.13 %
Acidity: 0.72 %
Fruit description: Flat, medium large, with a thick, often strigged stem. Skin is dull red over 70% of surface, on a yellow ground.
Blossom time: Early–mid-season bloom;
Flowering group: 4
Harvest time: Mid–late harvest
Chilling requirements: Normal
Other information: Tree form: a medium, slightly spreading, neat tree. A heavy cropper.

## BULMERS NORMAN

Synonyms: none known
Provenance: Originated in Normandy, France. Imported to England in early 1900s. Famously developed by H.P. Bulmer & Co. Ltd. in Hereford, UK.
Flavour type: bittersweet
Tannin: 0.27 %
Acidity: 0.24 %
Fruit description: Medium sized greenish-yellow conical apples with a slight orange flush. Diameter 2-1/4". Flesh white, woolly, sweet astringent. Used only for cider making.
Blossom time: Early bloom.

Flowering group: 3

Harvest time: Early/mid-season

Ploidy: Triploid. Pollination requires at least one fertile variety in the same flowering group to be within bee-range.

Chilling requirements: Normal

Other information: A very vigorous tree, large and spreading, strong grower, produces good crops. Tends to be biennial. Poor pollen. Fair tolerance to blight. Scab susceptible. Branches prone to breaking but very winter-hardy. Picked fruit keeps for up to three weeks in storage. Good juice for blending. Produces a fast-fermenting medium cider.

*Malus pumila 'Bulmer's Norman'.*
*Image: The Heritage Fruits Society, Australia.'*

## CALVILLE BLANC D'HIVER

The name translates as 'White Winter Calville' or 'Calville's White Winter'.

Synonyms: Blanche de Zurich, Calville blanc, Admirable blanche, A frire, Blanche des Wurtembergeois, Bonnet carré, Caleville de Gascogne, Caleville tardif, Calleville blanc à côtes, Calvine, Calvire, Cotogna, De Coing, Fraise d'hiver, Gros rambour à côtes, Grosse pomme de Zurich, Grosse pomme blanche du Wurtemberg, Melonne, Niger, Reinette à côtes, Reinette cotelée, Taponne, Tapounelle

Provenance: Dates back to the 1500's in Normandy, France.

Flavour type: sharp

Low tannin, high acid.

Fruit description: A gourmet French culinary apple. Medium-large irregular-shaped fruit, skin yellow to pale green, russeted, with light red dots on the sunny side. The fruit has appealing aromatic, tender, sweet, juicy flesh and exceptional, spicy flavour. It is a good juice apple with more vitamin C than an orange. The perfect choice for apple tarts and sauces. Apart from being a famous culinary apple, Calville blanc d'hiver is well known for making excellent cider.

'Most famous of all the Calville apples, probably the first one that created the term "Calville", which refers to the classic pentagonal ribbed shape of a calville apple when viewed from above the calyx. Most likely named after the town of Calleville in Normandy. Although now no longer much used in France, this used to be the top most desired cooking apple in France and in high demand by French chefs in England. Used to be espaliered around Paris to meet the culinary demand.'[4]

Blossom time: Mid—Late season

Flowering group: 4.

Harvest time: late

Ploidy: Triploid. Pollination requires at lest one fertile variety in the same flowering group to be within bee-range.

Pollinating partners: Most crab-apples will be good pollinators for this variety.

Chilling requirements: Normal chill

Other information: The tree is tip-bearing and a precocious bearer.

## CALVILLE ROUGE D'HIVER

The name translates as 'Red Winter Calville'.

Synonyms: General, Winter Red Calville, Cushman's Black. This apple has so many synonyms that we have listed only the most common ones on this page. The rest can be found at the end of the book.

Provenance: France. Very old variety, known since the seventeenth century. Probably originally Breton.

Flavour type: Sharp

Low tannin, high acid.

Fruit description: Medium to large apple with an oblong conical shape, and strong ribbing, with a pronounced crown. Skin background colour is greenish yellow beneath a mottled, washed-out red flush. Very little russetting. Flesh is crisp and fine, yellowish-white in colour and not very juicy.

---

4      *Calville Blanc D'Hiver—The Cloudforest Gardener Wiki. Accessed October 2013.*

Flowering group: 4.

Harvest time: late

Chilling requirements: Normal

Other information: The tree is a good producer but sensitive to canker. French descriptions mention a pink tinge to the flesh and a subtle raspberry aftertaste, but that appears to be a different apple with the same name.

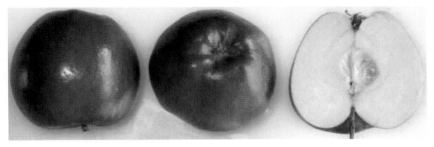

*Malus pumila 'Calville Rouge D'Hiver. Image: National Fruit Collection, UK*

## CHATAIGNIER

The name translates as 'Chestnut'.

Synonyms: De chastignier.

Provenance: An antique apple whose origin is unknown.

Flavour type: Sharp (but quite a sweet sharp)

Tannin: medium-high tannin and acid

Fruit description: Medium to large, spherical flattened, slightly conical. Skin is thin, smooth, almost entirely washed with pale yellow to dark orange, striped with carmine and speckled with gold dots. Flesh is white, crisp, sweet-tasting and pleasantly mellow. A nice eating apple and an excellent cooking apple.

Blossom time: Late.

Flowering group: 4—5

Harvest time: Late autumn to winter
Chilling requirements: Normal
Other information: Perfect for pies, tarts and cider.

*Malus pumila 'Chataignier'. Image: www.fruitiers.net*

## CIMETIERE DE BLANGY

The name translates as 'Blangy Cemetery'.
Synonyms: Cimetiere du pays, Cimetiere
Provenance: From the Pays d'Auge region in France,
    which is a major producer of Calvados, an apple
    brandy.
Flavour type: Bittersweet. Makes a sweet cider.
Tannin: 0.28
Acidity: 0.16
Fruit description: Irregularly shaped with greenish-
    yellow skin sometimes faintly blushed with orange,
    and some russetting.
Blossom time: Late season
Flowering group: 4
Harvest time: Late-ripening
Chilling requirements: Normal

Other information: Very specific varieties of cider apples from the Pays d'Auge, including Cimetière de Blangy, are often late-ripening and mostly bittersweet or bitter. After harvesting they are kept in barns for several weeks for further maturation.

## CLOZETTE

Synonyms: Closette
Provenance: Région de l'Avranchin in France
Flavour type: Sweet, but makes a dry cider.
Low tannin, low acid.
Fruit description: Medium sized fruit. Green with occasional red stripe over it, plus some fine russet. Pale yellow flesh. Also a wonderful eating apple.
Blossom time: medium to late.

Flowering group: 3

Harvest time: mid to late season

Triploid. Needs a pollinator for itself. Produces poor amounts of viable pollen.

Chilling requirements: Normal

## COURT OF WICK

Synonyms: Aniseed, Golden Drop, Glass of Wine.
Provenance: Originated at Court of Wick, Yatton, Somerset, England, and introduced to the market in 1790 by Wood of Huntingdon. Becoming more widely grown in the last half of the 19th century.[5]
Flavour type: Sharp. Makes good cider.
Low tannin, high acid.

---

5    'Court of Wick Apple Tree'. Heritage Fruit Trees, Victoria, Australia

Fruit description: Fruits are crisp with a rich and subacid fruity flavour. Aromatic tasting, highly flavoured, yellow flesh that can be rich and sweet.[6] Medium to small round, russet apple with an attractive yellow-gold skin, an orange flush and russet flecks with. A superb dessert apple.

Blossom time: Medium to late.

Flowering group 3

Harvest time: mid-season

Self sterile. Needs a pollinator for itself, produces viable pollen.

Chilling requirements: Normal

Other information: The tree is very hardy. A good keeping apple.

*Malus pumila 'Court of Wick'. Image: Victorian Nursery, UK*

---

6    *'Court of Wick'. Woodbridge Fruit Trees, Tasmania, Australia*

# COURT PENDU PLAT

Some say the name derives from the Old French 'corps pendu' ('hanging body'). Other believe it translates as 'Short Hanging Plate', perhaps referring to the fruit's short stem.

Synonyms: Also called 'Wise Apple' because it flowers very late and thus escapes late frost damage.

Provenance: France. An ancient variety, possibly dating from Roman times. Introduced to the French market in 1613 but believed to be much older than this.

Flavour type: Bittersweet

High tannin, low acid.

Fruit description: Skin is greenish-yellow becoming flushed with orange-red with short broken stripes. Rich, aromatic fruit with a good balance of sugar and acid.

Blossom time: late

Flowering group 6

Harvest time: late

Fertility: Self-sterile.

Chilling requirements: Normal

Other information: A good cropper

*Malus pumila 'Court Pendu Plat'. Image: Malus rustica*

# COURT ROYAL

Synonyms: Improved Pound, Sweet Blenheim, Possum (Australia). Not to be confused with Royal Court, a newer cultivar.

Provenance: Court Royal was found in East Devon, England.

Flavour type: Sweet. High sugar content. Fast-fermenting juice makes a light, sweet, vintage quality cider. Can be used to make a single variety cider described as 'A delicate medium dry cider'.

Low tannin, low acid.

Fruit description: Round conical shape, pale green skin with red stripes, soft, mealy flesh,

Blossom time: unknown

Flowering group 5

Harvest time: Late ripening

Ploidy: Triploid. Pollination requires at least one fertile variety in the same flowering group to be within bee-range.

Chilling requirements: Normal

Other information: Heavy crops, vigorous growth. Scab-susceptible. Dual-purpose dessert and cider variety with large fruit 5.7 cm diameter (2-1/4”).

# CRÉMIÈRE

Translates as 'Dairymaid'.

Synonyms: none known

Provenance: An old cider apple from Somerset, though the name suggests it might originally have been French.

Flavour type: Bittersweet

Tannin: Medium high

Acidity: Low.

Fruit description: medium sized elongated fruit, pale green to creamy colour. Crisp, sweet and quite pleasantly flavoured, with mild tannin, but not very juicy. A hard apple that stores well.

Blossom time: Mid to late season

Flowering group: 4—5

Harvest time: Late season

Chilling requirements: Normal

Other information: Crémière was recorded in the report of the Apple and Pear Conference of 1934 for the first and only time. Since then it became lost in the UK, possibly due to the mass devastation caused by fireblight. Fortunately this cultivar remained safe at Grove Research Station, Tasmania, from whence it was returned to Britain in 2005.

*Malus pumila 'Crémière'. Image: Bernwode Nurseries, UK*

# CIDER APPLES D TO H

*The Old Quining*

## DABINETT

Synonyms: Dabinette

Provenance: Somerset, UK

Flavour type: Bittersweet. A very high quality English cider variety, has been used to make a single variety cider. Makes a sweet, full-bodied cider.

Tannin: 0.29

Acidity: 0.18

Fruit description: A medium sized flattish red apple.

Blossom time: Late season

Flowering group: 4—6

Harvest time: Late harvest

Self-fertile. Produces viable pollen.

Chilling requirements: Normal

Other information: A good cropper. Some resistance to scab and fireblight. Most reliable bittersweet to grow. Precocious and very productive.

*Malus pumila 'Dabinett'. Image: Devon Apples UK*

## DE BOUTTEVILLE

Synonyms: De Bouteville, De Bouteveille.

Provenance: A seedling raised at Yvetot, France, by Monsieur Legrand. It first fruited in 1873, and was dedicated to Monsieur L. de Boutteville, Honorary President of the Societe Centrale d'Horticulture de la Seine Inferieure, and co-author of 'Le Cidre', published at Rouen, in 1875. This variety was introduced into Herefordshire by the Woolhope Club, in 1884.

Flavour type: Bittersweet. This apple is one of the best varieties for making a good cider that will keep well. The apple is firm in flesh, and travels well. Its juice is well coloured with excellent perfume and taste.

Tannin: High, Acidity: 2.14

Fruit description: of middle size, oblate, smooth and round, without angles. Skin: pale yellow, with an orange blush on the sunny side, more or less spotted over the surface, and the spots often become dark and tinged with red under the sun's influence. Eye: closed, seated in a narrow, deep cavity, with folded margins. Stalk: short, placed in a broad and deep cavity, lined with a thin russet that radiates over the base of the apple. Flesh: yellowish, with a sweet and pleasant flavour, free from bittterness. Juice is of a high colour, sweet, and pleasant.[7]

Blossom time: Early to mid season

Flowering group: 3

Harvest time: unknown

---

7     *Robert Hogg's 'The Apple & Pear as Vintage Fruits' (1886)*

Chilling requirements: Normal
Other information: This cider apple is mentioned by
    Hogg[8] as being among some of the best Norman
    apples introduced into Herefordshire:

'The apples they have selected are Rouge Bruyere,
Bramtot, Medaille d'or, Bedan-des-Parts, Michelin,
Argile grise, de Boutteville, and Frequin Audievre.
Trees of all these valuable varieties of true Norman
Apples have been sent to Messrs. Cranston and Co.,
King's Acre, Hereford, who will propagate carefully
from them. It is believed that they will prove very
valuable in the orchards of Herefordshire.'

## DELAPLACE

Synonyms: De la place
Provenance: From the Eure department in Brittany,
Flavour type: Sweet
Low tannin, low acid.
Fruit description: Fruit is variable in size. Skin has
    a pale yellow bloom on dark red-maroon skin.
    flavour is bitter and sweet. Good for eating fresh.[9]
Blossom time: midseason
Flowering group: 3
Harvest time: mid-season ripening
Chilling requirements: Normal
Other information: The De La Place cider apple
    cultivar in Australia has not yet been confirmed
    as being identical to the De La Place of France.

---

8    ibid
9    'Delaplace'. MiApple Heritage Apples, Victoria, Australia

## DOUX AMER GRIS

The name translates as 'Sweet-Bitter-Grey'.

Synonyms: Maigrillou, Doux d'amaigris, Douce amere grise.

Provenance: France. A basic variety of northern Ille-et-Vilaine especially in the region of Dol-de-Bretagne.

Flavour type: Bittersweet. The juice, which is of good density and well coloured, makes a red cider of excellent quality. The flavor is similar to that of a sweet wine. The apple is excellent for distillation into apple brandy.

High tannin, low acid.

Fruit description: A middle-sized, conical fruit. Skin background color is yellowish green overlaid with a red-orange wash. The fruits are often quite small.

Blossom time: late

Flowering group: 3

Harvest time: medium to late

Sometimes fertility is low. Bears best with a pollinator.

Chilling requirements: Normal

Other information: This is a good cooking apple. The juice is delicious. The tree is hardy and vigorous, very productive. The foliage is a unique pale grey/green colour. Doux Amer Gris was on the list of varieties recommended by the CFC (Comité des Fruits à Cidre) in 1949 and 1958, but was retired in 1966. There exists a more colourful red clone called 'Doux Amer Gris Rouge.'

## EGGLETON STYRE[10]

Synonyms: none known

Provenance: 'This apple was raised from the kernel by the late Mr. William Hill, at Lower Eggleton, Ledbury, Herefordshire, UK in the nursery attached to the farm. The seedling first bore fruit about the year 1847, and it was from the birds specially attacking the apple, that Mr. Hill's attention was directed to their sweet and rich flavour.'

Flavour type: Sweet. 'The Eggleton Styre makes excellent cider alone, very sweet and rich, with a high colour. It has been sold, fresh bottled. It fines better if mixed with Redstreak, Cowartie Red, Pym Square, Coolis Kernel, or Strawberry Hereford.'

Low tannin, low acid.

Fruit description: 'Middle sized, roundish, with obscure ribs on the sides. Skin: rich yellow, orange next to the sun, and covered with thin tracings and patches of russet. Stalk: slender, half an inch long, deeply inserted in a round cavity, which is lined with russet extending in branches over the base. Flesh: yellowish, tender, juicy, sweet and slightly acid.'

Blossom time: The middle of May in the UK

Flowering group: 4—6

Harvest time: early to midseason

Chilling requirements: Normal

Other information: 'The tree is hardy. It bears freely. The fruit is so sweet and aromatic as to be very attractive to hares, rabbits, fowls, blackbirds, and

---

10    *The Eggleton Styre information is chiefly from Robert Hogg's 'The Apple & Pear as Vintage Fruits' (1886)*

fieldfares, not to mention smaller birds. They will select this variety in preference to all others.' This cultivar was last officially recorded at the Apple and Pear Conference of 1934 and was afterwards lost to Britain, possibly due to the scourge of fireblight. The Grove Research Station, in Tasmania sent scions back to the UK in 2005.

*Malus pumila 'Eggleton Styre'. Image: Bernwode Nurseries, UK*

## FAMEUSE

Synonyms: American Nonpareil, Amerikanischer Schneeapfel, Chimney Apple, De neige, du Marechal, Feimez, Formosa, Frogmore Dessert, Hires alma, La belle fameuse, La fameuse, Neige, Neige-frambose de Gielen, Pomme de Fameuse, Pomme de neige, Pomme de neige der Amerikaner, Pomme de Niege, Pomme Fameuse, Pomme neige, Red American, Royal Snow, Sanguineous, Sanguineum, Sanguineus, Schneeapfel, Snejnoe,

Snow, Snow Apple, Snow Chimmey, Snow Chimney, Snow Apple of Quebec, Vytecne Jablko

Provenance: Thought to be a Canadian variety and may have been raised from seed brought from France by early settlers. It was planted in the USA in about 1730

Flavour type: Sweet.

Low tannin, low acid.

Fruit description: A small bright red-crimson apple with bright white 'snowy' flesh and a distinctive sweet taste. Fruits have rather soft, fine-textured, juicy flesh with a very sweet and vinous flavour—similar to McIntosh. Flesh texture is tender, soft and melting.

Blossom time: Early—Mid season

Flowering group: 3

Harvest time: Late season

Self-sterile and needs a pollination partner nearby.

Chilling requirements: Normal to high.

Other information: A very hardy apple variety. A heavy cropper, so thin out the apples early, while they are small, in order to get the best size and reduce the crop load. The tree has a biennial tendency. It has good disease resistance with the exception of being highly susceptible to scab. Apples keep for one to two months. Our ancestors made good use of this cultivar for cider because of its aromatic and distinct flavour, and because it is a fair to good keeper. Good for juice, cider, sauce, cooking and baking. Also an excellent dessert apple for eating fresh.

*Malus pumila 'Fameuse'. Image: Heritage Fruits Society.*

## FENOUILLET GRIS

The word 'fenouillet' means 'fennel', of which the apple's aniseed flavour is said to be reminiscent.

Synonyms: D'Anis, De fenouillet, D'epice d'hiver, Gorge de pigeon, Du ronduraut, D'anny, Petit fenouillet, Spice, Anizier, Aromatique russet, Caraway Russet, d'Anis, Annis, Anis, d'Anny, du Ronduraut, Epice d'hiver, Fenouillet, Fenouillet anisé, Fenouillet gris anisé, Fenouillet roux, Gros-fenouillet Gros-fenouillet d'or, Petit-fenouillet, Fenellet, Fenouillet, d'Or Gros, Porame d'anis, George de pigeon, Graue Fenchelapfel, Grauer Fenchelapfel. Anisapfel, Winter Auisreinette. (Also there are plenty of misspellings).

Provenance: France. An old apple first recorded in 1608 when described as Espice d'hiver ('Winter Spice'), listed by Olivier de Serre. Like most Fenouillets it is a native of Anjou. This cultivar was listed in the London Horticultural Society catalogue of 1826.

Flavour type: Sweet

Low tannin, low acid.

Fruit description: A good quality aromatic russet apple. Medium sized, roundish ovate, but broadest at the base. The skin is golden yellow nearly covered with brown russet, with a greyish brown tinge on the sunny side. The flesh is yellowish white, fine, firm, rich, tender, crisp and sugary with a fine sweet aniseed flavour, becoming tender and succulent at full maturity. This is a dessert apple that is also used for cider. If kept too long after picking, its flesh becomes woolly.[11]

Blossom time: Midseason

Flowering group: 2

Harvest time: March—April

Needs a pollinator for itself, produces viable pollen.

Chilling requirements: Normal

Other information: An excellent dessert apple which, when well ripened is considered of first-rate quality by those who are partial to its peculiar flavor. It is in season from December to March (northern hemisphere). The tree is a small and slender grower; but an abundant bearer. It requires a rich soil and warm situation, and succeeds well as a dwarf on the paradise stock. There has been some confusion between this apple and the similarly aniseed-flavoured Caraway Russet, starting with Lindley in the 1830s, and not entirely resolved. The nurserymen at Woodbridge Fruit Trees, Tasmania, say, 'This is the most unusual apple we grow.'

---

11    *'Fenouillet gris', Bernwode Fruit Trees, UK*

*Malus pumila 'Fenouillet Gris'. Image: Fruitiers. net*

## FRENCH CRAB

Synonyms: John Apple, Winter Greening, Easter Pippin, Ironstone Pippin, Iron King, Two Year's Apple, Amiens Long Keeper, Amiens Long-keeper, Claremont, Claremont Pippin, Green Beefing, Gruner Oster, Gruner Oster Apfel, Iron Stone Apple, Ironside, Ironsides, Ironstone, Robin, Somerset Stone Pippin, Three Years Old, Tunbridge Pippin, Winter Queening, Yorkshire Robin, Young's Long Keeper, Young's Long Keeping, Young's Long-Keeping.[12]

Provenance: Thought to have originated in France. It was brought to England at the end of the 1700s.

Flavour type: Bittersharp
High tannin, high acid.

Fruit description: Fruits have white, distinctly green tinged flesh which is very firm, coarse-textured and a little juicy and acid. It cooks well, having a strong aroma when cooking. Flesh is crisp. Medium size or perhaps small cooking size and very regular.

---

12    *'French Crab'. National Fruit Collection UK*

A completely round apple with flat ends, very hard and firm. Dark green with numerous small russet dots speckled over surface. Intense darker green around eye. Skin feels greasy. The cavity is fairly wide and fairly deep, the amount of russet varies. Acid in flavour and cooks to a sharp puree.

Blossom time: not known

Flowering group: 3

Harvest time: not known

Chilling requirements: Normal

Other information: Probably the mother to Granny Smith. Keeps well in storage.

*Malus pumila 'French Crab'. Image: National Fruit Collection*

# FOXWHELP

Synonyms: Fox-whelp, Foxwell, Old Foxwhelp.

Provenance: 'The Foxwhelp is a very old cider apple cultivar, originating in England. It was first recorded in 1653. Trees which provided the sample fruit depicted in the 'Herefordshire Pomona'[13] were believed to have been planted in about 1609, which if correct make this the earliest dated Gloucestershire apple variety.

'This is one of the oldest surviving varieties of cider apple; it is mentioned in John Evelyn's Advertisements Concerning Cider in his work 'Pomona' of 1664, in which it is commented that "cider for strength [...] is best made of the Fox-whelp of the Forest of Dean, but which comes not to be drunk until two or three years old".

'By the early eighteenth century, it had become one of the most prized cultivars for cider: a letter written by a Hugh Stafford in 1727 states "I have been told by a person of credit that a hogshead of cider from this fruit has been sold in London for £8 or eight guineas, and that often a hogshead of French wine has been given in exchange for the same quantity of Fox-whelp. It is said to contain a richer and more cordial juice than even the Red-streak itself".[14]

Flavour type: Bittersharp

---

13      'The Herefordshire Pomona is a 19th-century catalogue of the apples and pears that were grown in the county of Herefordshire in England.' Source: George Monbiot (2004—10-30). "Fallen fruit". The Guardian.

14      From 'Native Apples of Gloucestershire'—Gloucestershire Orchard Group and Robert Hogg's 'The Apple & Pear as Vintage Fruits' (1886)

Tannin: high

Acidity: high

Fruit description: A small to medium-sized fruit with a lop-sided, irregular, ridged/ribbed shape, hints of five-crowning and a brilliant crimson skin with yellow stripes. Its flesh is acidic and yellow with a red tinge. The side facing the sun is more crimson than on the shaded side. Russet virtually absent except in cavity. Susceptible to scab.

Flowering group: 2

Harvest time: early autumn

Chilling requirements: Normal

Other information: The Foxwhelp is prone to the disease apple scab.

Wikipedia says: 'Along with many other old varieties of apple, the Foxwhelp is now rare. Some sources state that many apples identified as Foxwhelp today are not, in fact, the original variety, which came to be known as "Old Foxwhelp" to distinguish it from later sports (such as "Improved Foxwhelp", developed by H. P. Bulmer), which were selected from the original cultivar.

'By the 1960s the Long Ashton Research Station could locate only "a few very old trees" of Old Foxwhelp in Herefordshire and Gloucestershire. However, the Gloucestershire Apple Collection did manage to secure cuttings for propagation from an orchard in Gloucestershire, which had been used by Long Ashton as a source of Foxwhelp propagating material until the 1950s.'

Hogg[15] suggested the name 'Foxwhelp' arose because it was a seedling found near a fox's earth, or possibly

---

15    *The Apple & Pear as Vintage Fruits', Robert Hogg' (1886)*

that a foxhunter discovered it, conspicuous because of its bright coloured fruit, and named it. There was even a suggestion that the eye of the fruit resembles the physiognomy of a fox cub. 'Foxwhelp' cider is reported always to have 'a peculiar aroma', possibly reminiscent of a fox's scent, and maybe this is what has given rise to its name.

Robert Hogg cautions apple-growers, "The Foxwhelp ... yields the Cider, so remarkable for its strength, and that peculiar flavour, for which it is so highly esteemed, from deep clay Sandstone loam, and if the trees are grown on light or too sandy a soil, its Cider is then thin and inferior in flavour. The same may be said of several other varieties.'

The Foxwhelp is prone to producing sports (mutations) on a given branch. This is possibly how some of the other 'Foxwhelp' varieties like 'Black Foxwhelp', 'Broxwood Foxwhelp', 'Red Foxwhelp' and 'Rejuvenated Foxwhelp' occurred, rather than as seedlings of the original.[16]

Hogg praises the Foxwhelp at length, with such phrases as 'the renowned Foxwhelp, first mentioned by Evelyn as coming from the Forest of Dean, and which has since surpassed all others in repute ... The Foxwhelp which has been the favourite apple for nearly two hundred years still lives and is propagated ...'

He adds,

'A supply of good Foxwhelp Cider, made in a good year, would have refreshed the warriors for twice, or thrice, or even four times the duration of the siege of Troy. It will retain its full flavour for twenty or thirty

---

16    Martell, C. Native Apples of Gloucestershire, Gloucestershire Orchard Group.

years, and a strength moreover, that would require
the three permitted glasses to be of moderate size.

'The Foxwhelp cider, when pure, is of great
strength, and always has a peculiar aroma, so marked
that it can be detected directly the cork is drawn from
the bottle. In taste, it is generally rough and strong,
with a peculiar vinous, musky flavour, which gives
its aroma. In ordinary seasons, unless made with
great care, it is not sweet enough to be acceptable
to strangers, and the taste which enjoys its peculiar
flavour fully, must in such circumstances, perhaps, be
acquired; but in a favourable year—a year of sunshine
and genial showers, when the fruit has been ripened
to perfection—happy is he who has a good hit of it.

*Malus pumila 'Foxwhelp'. Image: www.cider.org.uk*

'If he carries it well through the process of fermentation, and keeps the flavour of the fruit, and its sweetness too, he has cider in perfection—a cider that will sell readily in its own district, at a guinea a dozen; and a cider moreover, that will unquestionably improve in quality, for some three or four decades of years. It will not all be sold, however, for it is the pleasure and pride of the cider-growers of Herefordshire to have always ready for a friend, a bottle of good Foxwhelp cider of a good year.

'The juice of the Foxwhelp Apple is, however, most used to give strength and flavour to the cider of mixed fruit, and when this is well made, it is perhaps more generally popular than the very strong and pure Foxwhelp. A cider of this kind, excellent in quality, can be got at one shilling a bottle from the growers.

'At a public auction, a short time since (1880), at the late Mr. Mason's, Foxwhelp Cider was sold freely at 30s[hillings] the dozen, and Taynton Squash Perry fetched 28s. a dozen, at the same sale. Either of these varieties, and some others too, when of good age and of the first quality, will always command high prices. The Foxwhelp Cider from Mr. John Bosley, of Lyde, near Hereford, which won the First Prize at the Herefordshire Agricultural Society's Meeting at Ledbury, in 1884, sold quickly at £1 the dozen.

'The Foxwhelp beyond all question, in general estimation is the most valuable cider apple, and by intelligent perseverance in propagating it, it will long continue to be so.'

## FREQUIN ROUGE

Synonyms: none known.

Provenance: Brittany, France.

Flavour type: Bittersweet. Used to make Scrumpy.

Tannin: Very high

Acid: Low.

Fruit description: Medium globular to flat round in shape, yellow with medium red stripes no russet, flesh crisp and juicy.

Blossom time: Early to mid season

Flowering group: 3—4

Harvest time: Ripens mid to late season.

Chilling requirements: Normal

Other information:

This cider apple, 'rediscovered' in Australia, has not yet been verified as identical with any of the French cultivars, however the New South Wales Department of Primary Industries (Agriculture) believes it is part of the French 'Frequin Rouge cider apple' group. This group includes 'Frequin Red', 'Frequin Rouge Petit' 'Doux Fréquin Rouge de Rennes', 'Frequin Lajoie', 'Fréquin de la Méttrie' etc.

'The etymology of the word 'Frequin' is a mystery. Historic French literature gives many variants of this name, including: Freschin, Friquet, Fraisquin, Fréquet, Frétien, Fréchin... It could simply come from the name of somebody and not have any particular meaning...

'As for Frequin rouge... I have counted more than 40 varieties that have the word "Frequin" in Bore and Fleckinger's book! It could be almost any of them, with the name slightly modified in Australia.'[17]

---

17      *Claude Jolicoeur*

## GALOPIN[18]

Synonyms: Galopina, Petite douce rousse. 'Galopin' translates as 'kitchen boy'.
Provenance: Normandy, France
Flavour type: Sweet
Fruit description: The skin is light greenish yellow, sometimes with a blush on the side facing the sun. The flesh is sweet. Quite resistant to apple scab, quite sensitive to mildew, very susceptible to canker, quite resistant to fire blight.
Flowering group: 'D' in the French classification.
Harvest time: Late-maturing.
Chilling requirements: normal

## GOLDEN HARVEY

Synonyms: Bradley's Golden Pippin, Brandy, Brandy Apple, Guernsey Pippin, Harvey Dore, Harvey's Gold Apfel, Harvey's Goldapfel, Herefordshire Golden Harvey, Round Russet Harley, Round Russet Harvey, The Harvey Apple[19]
Provenance: Thought to have originated in the 1600s in Herefordshire UK
Flavour type: Bittersweet
High tannin, low acid.
Fruit description: Small, round, golden with red/orange blush covered in brown russett: flesh crisp, sweet acid. Fruits have firm, crisp, yellow flesh with a sweet, rich, aromatic flavour. A dual purpose dessert apple, one of the richest and best.
Flowering group: 2
Harvest time: unknown
Chilling requirements: Normal

---

18    *'Galopin'. Pommiers a Cidre, by Bore and Fleckinger. 1997*
19    *'Golden Harvey'. National Fruit Collection, UK.*

## GOLDEN HORNET

This is a true crabapple, meaning the fruit is small
and it belongs to an apple species other than
Malus pumila. Its botanical name is Malus x zumi
'Golden Hornet'. Like Hewe's Crab (unavailable in
Australia) it makes good cider.

Synonyms: none known

Provenance: Reported to be a seedling selection of
Malus toringo (syn. *M. sieboldii*).

Flavour type: Bittersharp. High tannin, high acid.
Used in cider making by Castle Hill Cider, Virginia
USA.

Fruit description: The tree bears very large quantities of small 1.3 cm (1/2 inch) yellow crabapples
in autumn. They stay on the tree until after leaf
fall. Excellent for cider. High in pectin, so also
excellent for crabapple jelly.

Blossom time: mid- to late-season.

Flowering group: 4—6. Much used as a pollenizer for
mid- and late-season blooming cultivars.

Harvest time: Very late.

Self fertile.

Chilling requirements: Normal

Other information: Highly ornamental. Deep pink buds
opening to single white flowers in mid-spring. It
has good resistance to apple scab, mildew and fire
blight. Annual bearing.

*Malus x zumi 'Golden Hornet'. Image: Pictokon*

## GRAVENSTEIN

Synonyms: Too many to list here! See back of book.

Provenance: Said to have originated either in the garden of the Duke of Augustenberg, Castle of Graefenstein, Schleswig-Holstein or in Italy or Southern Tyrol and sent to Schleswig-Holstein, or scions from Italy sent home by a brother of Count Chr. Ahlefeldt of Graasten Castle, South Jutland. It is thought to have arrived in Denmark in about 1669.[20]

Flavour type: Sharp. Low tannin, high acid.

Fruit description: Large apple with medium-strong ribbing, orange coloured skin. Flesh is crisp, rather coarse-textured, yellowish. Skin is a delicately waxy yellow-green with crimson spots and reddish lines. Flavour is pleasantly acid-sweet.

Flowering group: 2

Harvest time: early

Ploidy: Triploid

Chilling requirements: Normal

Other information: In Austria, Gravensteins are used for the production of high-quality brandy (Obstler). In Denmark the Food Minister proclaimed the Gravenstein to be the 'national apple'. Gravenstein is much used as a cooking apple. It does not keep well, so it is available only in season. In addition, their short stems and variable ripening times make commercial operations difficult. Apples tend to ripen individually over the course of a couple of weeks so you are not faced with a sudden glut. This lengthy ripening time is one of the reasons Gravenstein is not successful as a commercial variety, but is an advantage for the home orchardist.

---

20   *'Gravenstein'. National Fruit Collection, UK*

## Gros doux

The name translates as 'Big Sweet'.
Synonyms: Possibly 'Gros doux de France'
Provenance: France
Flavour type: Sweet
Tannin: Low, Acidity: Low
Fruit description: Large—weighing around 161g. Flat and round in shape. Green, white flesh crisp and juicy. Easily marked skin. Firm, crisp and juicy. Balanced and refreshing flavoured fruit. Fruit sugars—average 10.8%.
Blossom time: very late season
Flowering group: 4—5?
Harvest time: harvest in mid-season
Chilling requirements: Normal

## Groseille

The name translates as 'Gooseberry'.
Synonyms: None known
Provenance: Normandy, France
Flavour type: Sharp
Low tannin (1.24 g/L), high acid (5.8 g/L malic,)
Fruit description: A large fruit, yellow with red cheeks. The yellow flesh is slightly acidic.
Blossom time: unknown
Flowering group: 3
Harvest time: mid to late season
Chilling requirements: unknown
Other information: A dual-purpose cooking and cider apple. Note: the Groseille cider apple of Australia has not yet been confirmed as being identical with the Groseille of France.

# HOARY MORNING

Synonyms: Bachelor's Glory, Bedu Pteter Morgen Apfel, Bedufteter Morgenapfel, Blendon Seedling, Brouillard, Dainty, Dainty Apple, Downey, Downy, Downy Apple, General Johnson, Harmat alma, Harmat-alma, Honeymoon, Mela pruinosa, Morganduft Apfel, Morgenduft, Morgenduft Apfel, Morgenduftapfel, Morgendurft Apfel, Morgendust, New Margil, Pruhaty ploskoun, Sam Rawling's, Sam Rawlings, Utrennyaya rosa, Webster's Harvest Festival, Werbster Harvest Festival

Provenance: Thought to have been raised in Somerset, England. It was first recorded in 1819.

Flavour type: Bittersweet?

High tannin, low acid.

Fruit description: Medium oblate to flat and ribbed, pale green with pale red flush and stripes and russett near stem. Fruits have firm, rather coarse-textured, dry flesh which is not particularly acid and when eaten fresh has no flavour. It becomes sweeter with cooking and maintains its shape well.

Blossom time: mid-season

Flowering group: 3?

Harvest time: mid-season

Chilling requirements: Normal

Other information: very scab resistant

# CIDER APPLES I TO R

The Old Quining

## IMPROVED FOXWHELP

Synonyms: none known

Provenance: From Bulmers, Hereford, England, prior to 1920.

Flavour type: Bittersharp; produces an extremely bittersharp cider. Useful for cider blending.

High tannin, high acid.

Fruit description: Fruit shape is medium or large, conical or flattened fruit; irregular, almost closed eye and long stalk swollen at base in very shallow basin. Bright or dark red blush with stripe on skin. Gives an acidic and sweet juice.

Blossom time: Mid–late season bloom

Flowering group: 3

Harvest time: Early to mid- season

Needs a pollinator for itself, produces viable pollen

Chilling requirements: Normal chill

Other information: Another well-known variety developed by Bulmer's in Hereford, UK. A vigorous tree heavy with attractive pinkish-red apples, crops consistently. A medium to large upright tree; leaves characteristically curled or wavy.

## JAUNET

The name translates as 'Little Yellow'.

Synonyms: none known

Provenance: France

Flavour type: Bittersweet

High tannin, low acid.

Fruit description: small, round, yellow-green with russett.

Blossom time: mid-season

Flowering group: 3

Harvest time: mid-season
Chilling requirements: Normal
Other information: Tends to fruit biennially.

## KING DAVID

Synonyms: none known
Provenance: Discovered in 1893 by farmer Ben Frost, in a hedgerow in Washington County, Arkansas, USA. This cultivar was introduced in 1902 by Stark Brothers, Louisiana, USA. Thought to be a cross between Jonathan and Black Arkansas or Winesap.
Flavour type: Bittersharp. Ideal for cider.
Tannin: high
Acidity: high
Fruit description: a dessert apple also good for making sauces, pies and cider. Fruits have rather coarse flesh with a subacid, slightly sweet flavour. Skin is a very deep red colour over a yellow ground, the flesh is creamy yellow. Quite a spicy, tart, aromatic apple, similar to a winesap with a rich, vinous (wine-like) flavor. Exceptionally juicy. Red to dark black in colour, a good measure of astringency in the skin due to tannins.
Blossom time: Midseason
Flowering group: 4
Harvest time: ripens late.
Needs a pollinator for itself, produces viable pollen.
Chilling requirements: Useful in warmer areas, as it is relatively low-chill.
Other information: A heavy cropper. General disease resistance is good.

*Malus pumila 'King David'. Image: National Fruit Collection, UK*

## KING OF THE PIPPINS

Synonyms: See list at end of book
Provenance: France 19th century
Flavour type: Bittersweet:
High tannin, low acid.
Fruit description: Flavour is sweet and sharp. Flesh is white and juicy. Skin is yellow-green flushed with dark orange.
Blossom time: Mid-Late season
Flowering group: 4
Diploid. Partially self-fertile
Harvest time: Midseason
Chilling requirements: normal
Other information: Triple purpose dessert, culinary and cider apple. Keeping period: two months. When cooked, it becomes sweeter, though still tart, and the flesh turns yellow, remaining firm in texture.

# Kingston Black

Synonyms: none known

Provenance: Believed to be a Somerset apple and possibly raised at Kingston, near Taunton. This variety was introduced into Herefordshire c.1820 by Mr Palmer of Bollitree Estate, Weston-under-Penyard near Ross-on-Wye.

Flavour type: Bittersharp. Fruits produce a full bodied, excellent quality cider with a distinctive flavour. Can be used to make a single-variety cider. Thought by some to be the perfect cider variety

High tannin, high acid.

Fruit description: A dark red, almost black coloured apple. Medium to small, conical, yellow with dark red stripes. Not much russet.

Blossom time: midseason

Flowering group: 4

Harvest time: Mid to late harvest.

Needs a pollinator for itself, produces viable pollen.

Chilling requirements: Needs high chill to set fruit.

Other information: Trees are of medium size and have a spreading habit. Susceptible to scab.

*Malus pumila 'Kingston Black'. Image: National Fruit Collection, UK*

## MARTIN FESSARD

Synonyms: Martin Frossard
Provenance: France
Flavour type: Bittersweet
High tannin
Low acid.
Fruit description: Large, round to conical, yellow washed with pink and touches of russet. Flesh is sweet to bittersweet.
Blossom time: flowers early
Flowering group: 2
Harvest time: Ripens midseason
Chilling requirements: Normal

## MICHELIN

Synonyms: none known.
Provenance: This old popular cider apple was raised by M. Legrand of Yvetot, Normandy, France. It first fruited in 1872. It was named after M. Michelin of Paris, one of the original promoters appointed by the French Government for the study of cider fruits. Introduced into Herefordshire in 1884 by the Woolhope Naturalists' Field Club.
Flavour type: Bittersweet. Produces medium cider, and often used for blending.
High tannin, low acid.
Fruit description: A small to medium-sized yellow-green fruit with a pink flush.
Blossom time: Midseason
Flowering group: 4
Harvest time: mid-season
Partially self-fertile. Produces viable pollen
Chilling requirements: Normal chill

Other information: Michelin has been extensively
planted in the English west midlands since the
1920's and remains widely grown both there and
in Normandy.

*Malus pumila 'Michelin'. Image: Ashridge Trees.*

## NORTHERN SPY

Synonyms: King Apple, King's Apple, Severnui Raz-
vedchik, Severnui Shpion, Spaeher des Nordens,
Spaher des Nordens, Spy, "Northern Spie" or
"Northern Pie Apple.
Provenance: First grown in the seedling orchard of
Heman Chapin, at East Bloomfield, New York,
USA from seed brought from Salisbury, Con-
necticut, USA. It was raised in about 1800 and
introduced in 1840.
Flavour type: Sharp. Eve's Cider's website states:
'Salty, citrusy, and dry, Northern Spy single
variety cider has tiny bubbles and a mouth-water-
ing acidity.'
Low tannin, high acid
Fruit description: Fruits have fairly firm, flesh with a
pleasant flavour. The white flesh is juicy, crisp and

mildly sweet with a rich, aromatic subacid flavor, noted for high vitamin C content. Its characteristic flavor is more tart than most popular varieties, and its flesh is harder/crunchier than most, with a thin skin. Skin color is a green ground, flushed with red stripes where not shaded,

Blossom time: Very late season

Flowering group: 4

Harvest time: late

Self-sterile and needs a pollination partner nearby.

Chilling requirements: Normal

Other information: This variety is resistant to woolly aphis and has been used as a parent in the breeding of resistant rootstocks and varieties. Northern Spy is commonly used for desserts and pies, but is also used for juices and cider. Further, the Northern Spy is also an excellent apple for storage, as it tends to last longer due to late maturation. Apples can be stored up to three months in a cool dry place lasting well into early spring.

*Malus pumila 'Northern Spy'. Image: National Fruit Collection, UK*

## Pomeroy of Somerset

Synonyms: Taunton, The Old Pomeroy, Jenny Oubury,
Old Pomeroy, Pome-roy, Pomeroy, Sweet Pomeroy.
Provenance: Originated in the UK. First described
in 1851.
Flavour type: Sweet.
Low tannin, low acid.
Fruit description: Medium sized, 7 cm (2 3/4 inches)
wide, and the same in height; conical, and obtusely
angular. Skin, greenish yellow, covered with thin
grey russet on the shaded side, but orange, striped
with deep red, and marked with patches of russet
on the side exposed to the sun, and strewed all
over with numerous large dark russety dots. The
stalk is short, and inserted in a round, even, and
russety cavity. Flesh is yellow, firm, crisp, juicy,
sweet, and highly flavoured. An excellent dessert
apple.[21]
Blossom time: Midseason
Flowering group: 4
Harvest time: late

*Malus pumila 'Pomeroy of Somerset'. Image: National Fruit Collection, UK*

---

21     *'The Fruit Manual', by Robert Hogg 1884*

# Red Cluster

Synonyms: none known

Provenance: Devon or Somerset, UK. It was recorded in 1884, though its true age is unknown.

Flavour type: Bittersweet

High tannin, low acid.

Fruit description: Small to medium sized red apples. The apples are very closely clustered and colour up bright red quite early in the summer. The flesh is sweet and without much acidity. A perfectly pleasant dessert apple, with sweet crisp and juicy flesh – and not unpleasantly tannic, but clearly of cider quality.

Blossom time: unknown

Flowering group: 4

Harvest time: late season

Chilling requirements: Normal

Other information: Red Cluster was assumed to be extinct in Britain until it was rediscovered at the Grove Research Station, Tasmania and new grafts were returned to England in 2005.[22] Trees spur freely and fruit abundantly when young.

# Red Normandy

Synonyms: 'Normandie Rouge'.

In his book 'All about Apples', Allan Gilbert suggests that the apple known in Australia as 'Red Normandy' may really be 'Blenheim Orange', a

---

22    *'Red Cluster'. Bernwode Nurseries, UK*

triploid, culinary apple which has a greenish-yellow to orange skin streaked with red. Against that argument is the fact that Blenheim Orange is listed as being in Australian Flowering Group 3.

The UK Apple and Pear Research Council lists Red Norman / Red Hereford as a cultivar, however it is as yet unproven whether this is in fact the Australian Red Normandy.

Fruit description: Large and flat with an orange blush and russet.

Flowering group: 4

## REINE DES HÂTIVES

The name translates as "Queen Hasty,' a title bestowed because this apple is an early ripener.

Synonyms: Sometimes misspelled as 'Reine de Hatives'.

Provenance: Raised in 1872 by Monsieur Dieppois, Yvetot, France. Introduced to the UK in the 1920s by Dr H.E. Durham and was distributed by H.P. Bulmer & Co.

Flavour type: Mild bittersweet.

Medium tannin, low acid.

Fruit description: A small to medium conical apple, skin yellow with a pink flush.

Blossom time: Mid–late season bloom

Flowering group: 3—4

Harvest time: Early harvest, giving a fairly good yield.

Self-sterile. Needs a pollination partner nearby.

Chilling requirements: Normal

Other information: A biennial but precocious cropper.

## RHODE ISLAND GREENING

Synonyms: Bell Dubois, Burlington Greening, Ganges,
    Green Newtown Pippin, Green Winter Pippin,
    Greening, Greenling von Rhode Island, Grunling
    von Rhode Island, Grunling von Rhode-Island,
    Hampshire Greening, Island's Grunling, Jersey
    Greening, Lindley Green Newton Pippin, Pomme
    Verte de Rhode-Island, Reinette du Seeland, Rhode
    Island, Rhode Island (Greening), Rhode-Island
    Greening, Russine, Seelander Reinette, Serinkia,
    Verte de Ile de Rhodes, Verte de l'Ile de Rhodes,
    Verte de Rhode Island, Verte de Rhode-Island,
    Zelence Rhodoislandske, Zelenka Rod-Ailend
    skaya.

Provenance: The Rhode Island Greening is an old,
    historic American apple variety and the official
    fruit of the state of Rhode Island. allegedly origi-
    nated around 1650 near Green's End in Newport,
    Rhode Island (in modern day Middletown).

The first Greenings were allegedly grown by a Mr.
Green who operated a tavern and developed apple
trees from seed. Green gave many scions from the
tree to visitors for grafting elsewhere, and the
original tree died. The apples became known as
Green's Inn apples from Rhode Island. One of the
oldest surviving trees was located on Mt. Hygeia
farm in Foster, Rhode Island at the turn of the
twentieth century.[23] The Rhode Island Greening

---

23     'The Apples of New York,' by Spencer Ambrose Beach,
Nathaniel Ogden Booth, Orin Morehouse Taylor. New York
(State) Dept. of Agriculture, New York State Agricultural
Experiment Station, 1905.

was one of the most popular apples grown in New York in the nineteenth century.[24]

Flavour type: sharp

Fruit sugars—average 11.5%

Fruit acids—average

Low tannin, high acid.

Fruit description: Very large (178g) with a flat, globose shape, strong ribbing. The skin is slightly greasy, its ground colour is whitish-yellow with a small amount of washed-out brown over-colour. Prone to extensive fruit russet. Flesh is yellowish and fine-grained, firm, crisp and juicy, good flavoured

Blossom time: early season

Flowering group: 3

Harvest time: Late season

Self sterile. Needs a pollination partner nearby.

Chilling requirements: Normal. Does not do well in warmer climates.

Other information: A good keeper. Prized for pie-baking in the 1800s. Used for eating, cooking, baking, cider and also good for drying.

## Rousse Latour

Named after a Monsieur Latour.

Synonyms: Rous Latour, Rousse-Latour

Provenance: France

Flavour type: Sweet

Low tannin, low acid.

Fruit description: Small to medium apple with a conical oval to long shape, yellow skin with a blush on the sunny side and russeted.

---

24    *Cyclopedia of American Horticulture, by Liberty Hyde Bailey, Wilhelm Miller Edition: 2, 1902.*

Blossom time: medium to late
Flowering group: 4
Harvest time: very late
Chilling requirements: Normal

*Malus pumila 'Rousse Latour'.*
*Image: NSW Department of Primary Industries*

## ROXBURY RUSSETT

Note: The identity of the apple cultivar in Australia
known as 'Roxbury Russet' is still unconfirmed.
Synonyms: none known.
Provenance: The Roxbury Russet is believed to be the
oldest apple cultivar bred in the United States,
having first been discovered and named in the
first half of the 17th century in the former Town
of Roxbury, part of the Massachusetts Bay Colony
southwest of (now part of) Boston.[25]
Flavour type: sweet

---

[25]      *University of Massachusetts Cold Spring Orchard. Accessed December 2011.*

Low tannin, low acid.

Fruit description: A medium sized apple. Skin colour is yellow-gold, with a bronze blush and some russet. Flesh is coarse, pale yellow-cream to white with a very good sweet, subacid flavour. Very juicy.

Blossom time: Mid—Late season

Flowering group: 2—3

Harvest time: very late season

It is self-sterile and needs a pollination partner nearby.

Chilling requirements: Normal

Other information: Good for eating fresh, cooking, juice or cider. Keeps for three months or more in cool storage. The tree is a good cropper and a partial tip-bearer. Very resistant to scab, fireblight and cedar apple rust.

# CIDER APPLES S TO Z

The Old Quining

## Somerset Redstreak

This apple should not be confused with the Redstreak, a much older English cultivar.

Synonyms: none known.

Provenance: Sutton Montis, Somerset, UK. 1900—1949

Flavour type: Bittersweet. It is quite a mild bittersweet, however; probably the French would classify it as 'douce amere'. Perry's use this apple to make a single variety cider.

High tannin, low acid.

Fruit description: Medium, flat, conical fruit with a short stalk. A bright red apple with a slightly darker stripe. Very good flavour.

Blossom time: Mid-season

Flowering group: 3

Harvest time: It ripens slightly ahead of the main late-season cider varieties.

Not self-fertile. Needs a pollinator for itself, produces viable pollen.

Chilling requirements: Normal chill

Other information: Somerset Redstreak is one of the main commercial cider varieties planted in England. The tree is slightly prone to biennial bearing, fruiting more heavily in alternate years. This can be controlled by heavier thinning in the "on" year.

*Malus pumila 'Somerset Redstreak'.*
*Image: NSW Department of Primary Industries*

## STAYMAN'S WINESAP

Synonyms: Winesap (false), Stayman, Stayman Winesap

Provenance: Developed in 1866 by Joseph Stayman of Leavenworth, Kansas, USA and sold by nurseries from 1895.[26] An improvement on its parent, Winesap. Mr Stayman planted a seed from a Winesap apple, and then tended the tree long enough to discover that it bore remarkably flavourful fruit. The tree it turned out to be "more productive and adapted to a much wider range of soil[s] and climate[s]" than even the parent tree.[27]

---

26     *Stayman (apple). Wikipedia. Accessed October 2013.*
27     *Apples: Old and New. U. P. Hedrick & George Henry 1913*

The chief differences in fruit quality between offspring and parent is that Stayman's Winesap is larger than Winesap, and is generally regarded as the more flavourful. But it is also less brilliantly colored, even dull, and must be grown with a pollinator variety such as Golden Delicious, Grimes, or Winter Banana, or Gala, to set fruit at all.[28]

Flavour type: Bittersweet

High tannin, low acid

Fruit description: Stayman is a medium-sized, roundish-conical apple with a thick greenish-yellow skin covered almost entirely with a deep red blush, darker red stripes and russet dots. The stem cavity often shows heavy russeting. Firm, tender, finely-textured juicy, crisp yellowish-green flesh is aromatic, tart and spicy. This apple is highly renowned for its excellent rich, delicious vinous (wine-like) flavour. A dual purpose dessert and cider apple.

Blossom time: Mid—late season

Flowering group: 4—6

Harvest time: late

Triploid. Produces no viable pollen and needs a pollination partner nearby.

Chilling requirements: Suits temperate climates. Fairly low chill.

Other information: Stayman's Winesap apples keep very well.

---

28    *Tim Hensley, Rood Remarks, 'Winesap of Stayman?' 2012*

*Malus pumila 'Stayman's Winesap'. Image: KCRW Good Food*

## STOKE RED

Synonyms: Stoke's Red, Stokes Red, Neverblight.

Provenance: This variety gained attention in the 1920s when surveys found trees growing in Rodney Stoke, Somerset. (Rodney Stoke is a town, not a man!)

Flavour type: Medium bittersharp. Produces a sharp, slightly astringent juice and a fine, sharp cider. Widely considered one of the highest quality English cider apple varieties.

G. Watkin Cider Company, UK, makes a single variety Stoke Red cider. They say, 'This popularity is a result of it being a good apple to sweeten, well bodied and with a good flavour. The cider produced from this apple takes a long time to ferment, which makes the cider late to mature.'

Tannin: high

Acidity: high

Fruit description: Small flat, round in shape. A yellow ground overlaid with dark red stripes. Cream coloured flesh.

Blossom time: very late

Flowering group: 5—7

Harvest time: Mid to late season

Partially self-fertile. but would require a pollinator to
produce a good crop. Produces viable pollen.

'If two trees with different flowering times are
growing close together,' Peter Cooke wrote in 2013,
'they often flower together. I notice this particularly in my potted tree nursery. I have Stokes Red
(usually week 7) growing beside Vérité (week 6)—
they both flowered together in week 9 last season.'
Seemingly, the trees' close proximity to each other
induced them to flower together. Vérité may prove
a suitable pollinator.

Chilling requirements: Needs high chill to set fruit.

Other information: The trees are fairly vigorous and
crop quite heavily

*Malus pumila 'Stoke Red'. Image: Dorset Cider*

## STURMER PIPPIN

Synonyms: Apple Royal, Creech Pearmain, Moxhay, Pearmain de Sturmer, Pepin de Sturmer, Pepin iz Shturmera, Royal, Sturner's Pepping, Sturmer, Sturmer Pepping, Sturmer's Pippin, Sturmers Pepping

Provenance: Ribston Pippin x Nonpareil. Raised by nurseryman Dillistone at Sturmer, Suffolk, England. First recorded in 1831.

Flavour type: Sweet. Very popular in Tasmania for making cider.

Low tannin, low acid.

Fruit description: Medium in size, medium amount of ribbing, oblong-conical in shape. Skin has a yellow ground with a brown-pink flush Flesh colour is greenish. Fruits have very firm, fine-textured, juicy flesh with a little subacid and rich aromatic flavour. A dual purpose dessert and cider apple.

Blossom time: Mid season

Flowering group: 4

Harvest time: late

Partially self-fertile but a nearby pollination partner is beneficial.

Chilling requirements: Normal

Other information: One of the best English keeping apples, Sturmer Pippin became widely grown and exported from Tasmania and New Zealand from the 1890s.[29]

---

29    *Morgan, J. & Richards, A. (Illus. Dowle, E.) (2002), The New Book of Apples.*

Mother to Oxford Hoard, Merton Russet, King's Acre Pippin, High View Pippin. Father to Ball's Pippin, Merton Pippin.

Sturmer Pippin's flavour improves after a few weeks in storage.

## SUGAR-LOAF PIPPIN

Synonyms: Sugarloaf Pippin, der Zuckerhut Apfel, Dolgoe Skvoznoe, Dolgoi Scusznoi, Dolgoi Skrasnoi, Dolgoi Skvoznoe, Dolgoi Squoznoi, Dolgoit Squoznoie, Dymond's Sugar Loaf, Hutchin's Seedling, Hutching's Seedling, Hutchings' Seedling, Hutchins' Seedling, Langer Durchsichtiger, Langer Durchsichtiger Apfel, Pain de Sucre, Pain de Suere, Pan di Zucchero, Reinette Pain de Sucre, Saharnaya Golova, Sugar Loaf Greening, Sugar Loaf Pippin, Zuckerhut Apfel

Provenance: 'Mr Hutchings was a market gardener in Kensington at the start of 19th century. He may have introduced it from its home in St. Petersburg, Russia. It was in the first catalogue of fruits at the London Horticultural Society's garden at Chiswick, Middlesex, in 1826. Dolgoi means long, Squoznoi means transparent, amply describing the apple.'[30]

Flavour type: Sharp

Tannin: low, Acidity: high

Fruit sugars—low 8.6%

Fruit description: Fruit size—small, around 91g. The shape is long and narrow, ovate-oblong. Skin is pale yellow with greenish dots, and on the sunny side

---

30    *Sugar-loaf Pippin. Apple descriptions, Bernwode Fruit Trees UK*

becoming nearly white when ripe. The flesh is firm, juicy, refreshing and crisp with a most agreeable lively, sweetish sub-acid flavour. Although all the historic writers acknowledge it is sweetish, they all classify it as culinary, the sweetness and uncooked flavour not being sufficient to consider it dessert, despite its name. In fact, if caught just right, it is most delicious to eat. Blossom time: Late season

Flowering group: 3—4

Harvest time: very early season

Needs a pollinator for itself, produces viable pollen.

Chilling requirements: Normal

Other information: 'A culinary and eating apple that doesn't keep. An old variety, "lost" in Britain [probably after the introduction of fireblight] and the subject of some detective work to rediscover it. Bernwode Fruit Trees retrieved Sugar-loaf Pippin from both Belgium and Woodbridge Fruit Trees in Tasmania.'.[31]

*Malus pumila 'Sugar-Loaf Pippin'. Image: OAK Tasmania Tahune Fields*

---

31      *ibid*

## Summer Stibbert

Synonyms: Stubbard, Avant Tout, Avant Tout Hative, Avant Toute Hative, Hative, Hative Pomme, Stibbert, Summer Queening, Stubbard-Hattie.
The French synonyms such as 'Hasty Before All', indicate the early ripening characteristics of this apple.

Provenance: Originated in the West of England. Recorded in 1831.

Flavour type: Sharp. A dual purpose dessert and cider apple. Dorset Cider states: 'Our Stubbard cider sample made in 2007 was rated as "Rather woody tasting, sharp cider, lacking body but would be good for blending." As a very early maturing apple, Stubbard might be included in the first, early cider made in the season, when it would contribute useful sharpness and some sugar.'

Tannin: 0.17%, Acidity: 0.83%

Fruit description: Fruits have firm, tender, creamy white flesh with a slightly subacid flavour. An unusual looking apple. The knobbly pale yellow fruit has distinct ribs rising to a crowned and furrowed nose. The stem is long and thick and projects distinctly. (*Source: Dorset Cider*)

Blossom time: Midseason

Flowering group: 3

Harvest time: early

Chilling requirements: Normal

Other information: Orchardist Peter Cooke notes: 'The Australian (Grove Heritage Nursery, run by OAK Tasmania) version of this apple is yellow with heavy red flush/stripes—I doubt if it is the same variety [as the one in Mr Cooke's collection].'

The Grove apple seems likely to be the old Michael-mas Stubbard—see endnote.*

*Malus pumila 'Summer Stibbert'. Image: Dorset Cider*

## SWEET ALFORD

Synonyms: none known.

Provenance: From Devon, England.

Flavour type: Mild bittersweet. Produces good quality cider. Llanblethian Orchards UK makes a single variety cider from Sweet Alford, described as 'a light, very sweet cider with some bitterness.' Also excellent for cider blending.

Medium tannin, low acid.

Fruit description: Medium size, flat and conical in shape. Skin is waxy and green to yellow with a diffuse pinkish-orange flush. Flesh is white, slightly crisp and sweet, with no astringency.

Blossom time: Mid-season

Flowering group: 4

Harvest time: Mid-season

Sweet Alford is self-sterile and requires a pollinator to produce a crop.

Chilling requirements: Normal
Other information: The fruit keeps in storage for more than three weeks. Large, tip-bearing tree with a slightly spreading habit. A good cropper. Due to its sweetness Sweet Alford also doubles as an excellent juicing apple.

## SWEET COPPIN

Synonyms: none known.
Provenance: An old variety originating in Devon, UK. Once very common in cider orchards in the Exeter area.
Flavour type: Sweet. Produces a pure sweet, sometimes a very mild bittersweet cider of good quality. Good for balancing with sharp and bittersharp varieties. Has been used to make a single variety cider, but it is sweet with no astringency.
Low tannin, low acid.
Fruit description: Medium to large fruits, conical green-yellow with slight orange-pink flush.
Blossom time: Midseason
Flowering group: 4
Harvest time: Late midseason
Self fertile but yield increases with nearby pollinators.
Chilling requirements: Normal
Other information: Susceptible to mildew. Precocious and productive. Tends to be biennial.

*Malus pumila 'Sweet Coppin'. Image: Rockingham Forest Cider*

## TARDIVE DE LA SARTHE

The name translates as 'Late Sarthe'.

Synonyms: Frequin tardive de la Sarthe, Frequin tardive de Sarthe, Tardive de la Sarth, Frequin tardif de la Sarthe.

Provenance: Sarthe, France. Sarthe is a French department, named after the Sarthe River. It was created in 1790, during the French Revolution. The history of the region dates back to Roman times.

Flavour type: Bittersweet

High tannin, low acid.

Fruit description: A small to medium fruit, round to conical in shape with strong ribbing. The skin has a yellow ground with a faint orange striped/solid flush. Medium juiciness.

Blossom time: late,

Flowering group: 6

Harvest time: late

Chilling requirements: Normal

Other information: Susceptible to fireblight.

## TREMLETT'S BITTER

Synonyms: none known.

Provenance: Originated in the Exe Valley, Devon. UK

Flavour type: Bittersweet. Sheppy's Cider of Taunton, England, makes a single variety Tremlett's Bitter Cider said to be 'rich in flavour and medium/ dry in taste'. If you prefer something sweeter, blend Tremlett's with a sweet cider apple such as Dabinett to make a delightfully flavoursome cider.

High tannin, low acid.

Fruit description: A small to medium-sized apple with a globose, conical shape and medium ribbing. The skin's background colour is green-yellow, mostly mottled with orange stripes and splashes. The flesh is white with a bitter flavour.

Blossom time: Very early

Flowering group: 4

Harvest time: Late-season

Tremlett's Bitter is self-sterile and needs to be pollinated by another tree of a different variety nearby.

Pollinating partners: 'Possibly Brown's Apple and Yarlington Mill may be early enough to pollinate, otherwise dessert varieties like Granny Smith and Jonathan would do well.'[32]

Chilling requirements: Normal

Other information: Flowers are very sensitive to frost which may contribute to the trees biennial cropping pattern. Medium sized, semi-spreading, precocious tree; a good cropper.

---

32      *Cider apple variety: Tremlett's Bitter. NSW Department of Primary Industries.*

*Malus pumila 'Tremlett's Bitter'. Image: Ornamental Trees UK*

## VÉRITÉ

The name translates as 'Truth'.
Synonyms: none known
Provenance: Originated in France. Recorded in 1876
Flavour type: Sharp
Low tannin, high acid.
Fruit description: A medium sized apple with a broad, globose conical shape. The skin has some red stripes over a green-yellow ground and some russet. The flesh is firm, crisp and juicy. Greenish in colour with a slightly sweet, subacid flavour.
Flowering group: 5—9
Harvest time: late
Pollinating partners: As mentioned previously, orchardist Peter Cook noticed that 'If two trees with different flowering times are growing close together, they often flower together.' He had Stokes Red (usually week 7) growing beside Vérité (week 6)—they both flowered together in week 9.'
Seemingly, the trees' close proximity to each other induced them to flower together. Stoke Red may prove a suitable pollinator. Normal chill.

## WINESAP

Synonyms: Virginia Winesap, American Wine Sop, American Wine-Sop, American Winesop, Banana, Henrick's Sweet, Holland's Red Winter, Pot Pie Apple, Potpie Apple, Red Sweet Wine Sop, Royal Red, Royal Red of Kentucky, Texan Red, Wine Sap, Wine Sop, Winesop, Winter Winesap

Provenance: From the eastern United States, introduced between 1800—1849

Flavour type: Bittersharp: High tannin, high acid. The Blue Mountain Cider Company and the Albemarle Ciderworks use Winesap to make a single varietal cider that has a 'dry refreshing finish, with a hint of tart apple taste.'

Fruit description: a medium to large red skinned apple. Flesh is firm, crisp and juicy, with a very good wine-like, aromatic, tart flavor.

Blossom time: Mid season

Flowering group: 3

Harvest time: Late season

Ploidy: Triploid. Self-sterile

Chilling requirements: Suits temperate climates

Other information: a tart small apple, and like many US heirloom varieties, keeps well in cold storage; three months or more. A good cropper. Uses: culinary and dessert apple, juice, sauce. Good disease resistance.

## YARLINGTON MILL

Synonyms: Yarlington Mills

Provenance: Yarlington, North Cadbury, Somerset, England.

Flavour type: Bittersweet. Produces a medium vintage cider. A very good cider apple.

Low tannin, low acid.

Fruit description: Attractive elongated pink-yellow apples. A medium sized fruit with a lightly striped dark red skin; smooth and slightly waxy. Flesh is white, reddish below skin, slightly crisp with some astringency.

Blossom time: Mid–late bloom,

Flowering group: 3—4

Harvest time: late

Partially self-fertile, produces viable pollen.

Chilling requirements: Normal chill

Other information: A strong growing tree, tends to be biennial. Medium, semi-spreading, precocious tree; some scab susceptibility. Distinctive large, dark green leaves. A good cropper, fruit keeps more than three weeks in cool storage.

*Malus pumila 'Yarlington Mill'. Image: Ornamental Trees UK*

# YATES

Synonyms: Jates, Red Warrior, Yates Winter

Provenance: It originated with Matthew Yates of Fayette County, Georgia, USA about 1844.

Flavour type: Sweet. 'Aromatic' is how Bull Run Cider describes it.

Low tannin, low acid.

Fruit description: Fruit small, skin a pale yellow-red with some dark red stripes and flushes. Flesh is white, tender, juicy, aromatic, mildly subacid and often stained red just under the skin.[33] Flavour is sweet, aromatic and pleasant.

Blossom time: Early

Flowering group: 3

Harvest time: very late

Ploidy: Diploid

Chilling requirements: can tolerate low chill.

Other information: Yates is a famous American cider apple prized for the excellent cider it produces. Yates stores exceptionally well and its sweet flavour makes it an excellent apple for fresh eating. It is necessary to thin the fruit early, to increase the fruit size.

*Malus pumila 'Yates'. Image: Century Farm Orchards*

---

33    *'Yates'. Century Farm Orchards, USA*

# TABLE OF CULTIVARS

─────────❦─────────

ORDERED BY FLAVOUR TYPE,
WITH INFORMATION ABOUT HARVEST SEASON,
FLOWERING GROUP AND USES.

| FLAVOUR TYPE | NAME | HARVEST SEASON | FLOWER GROUP | DES-SERT | CULI-NARY | OTHER USES |
|---|---|---|---|---|---|---|
| bittersharp | Foxwhelp | early | 2 | | | |
| bittersharp | Breakwell's Seedling | early | 5 self-fertile | D | C | juice |
| bittersharp | Improved Foxwhelp | early to mid | 3 | | | |
| bittersharp | Winesap | late | 3 | D | C | juice; keeps well |
| bittersharp | King David | late | 4 | | | |
| bittersharp | Golden Hornet | late | 4 - 6 | | C | |
| bittersharp | Kingston Black | mid to late | 4 | | | |
| bittersharp | French Crab | unknown | 3 | | C | keeps well |
| bittersharp (medium) | Stoke Red | mid to late | 5 - 7 | | | |
| bittersweet | De Boutteville | early to mid | 3 | | | juice; keeps well |
| bittersweet | Bulmer's Norman | early to mid | 3 triploid | | | keeps well |
| bittersweet | Yarlington Mill | late | 3 - 4 | | | keeps well |
| bittersweet | Cimetiere de Blangy | late | 4 | | | |
| bittersweet | Tremlett's Bitter | late | 4 | | | |
| bittersweet | Red Cluster | late | 4 | D | | |
| bittersweet | Stayman's Winesap | late | 4 - 6 | D | C | keeps well |
| bittersweet | Crémière | late | 4 - 5 | | | |
| bittersweet | Dabinett | late | 4 - 6 | | | |

| FLAVOUR TYPE | NAME | HARVEST SEASON | FLOWER GROUP | DES-SERT | CULI-NARY | OTHER USES |
|---|---|---|---|---|---|---|
| bittersweet | Brown Snout | late | 5 self-fertile? | | | |
| bittersweet | Tardive de la Sarthe | late | 6 | | | |
| bittersweet | Court Pendu Plat | late | 6 self-sterile | D | | |
| bittersweet | Jaunet | mid | 3 | | | |
| bittersweet | Hoary Morning | mid | 3? | | C | |
| bittersweet | King of the Pippins | mid | 4 | D | C | juice; keeps well |
| bittersweet | Michelin | mid | 4 | | | |
| bittersweet | Martin Fessard | mid season | 2 | | | |
| bittersweet | Doux amer gris | mid to late | 3 | C | | juice |
| bittersweet | Somerset Redstreak | mid to late | 3 | D | C | |
| bittersweet | Frequin rouge | mid to late | 3 - 4 | | | |
| bittersweet | Bedan des parts | mid to very late | 4 diploid | | | |
| bittersweet | Golden Harvey | unknown | 2 | D | C | |
| bittersweet (mild) | Reine des Hâtives | early | 3 - 4 | | | |
| bittersweet (mild) | Sweet Alford | mid | 4 | | | juice; keeps well |
| sharp | Gravenstein | early | 2 triploid | D | C | juice |
| sharp | Summer Stibbert | early | 3 | D | | |

| FLAVOUR TYPE | NAME | HARVEST SEASON | FLOWER GROUP | DES-SERT | CULI-NARY | OTHER USES |
|---|---|---|---|---|---|---|
| sharp | Blanchet | early | 4 - 5 diploid | D | | |
| sharp | Sugar-loaf Pippin | early (very) | 3 - 4 | D | C | |
| sharp | Baldwin | late | 2 triploid | D | C | juice; keeps well |
| sharp | Rhode Island Greening | late | 3 | D | C | drying; juice; keeps well |
| sharp | Northern Spy | late | 4 | | C | root-stock; juice |
| sharp | Chataignier | late | 4 - 5 diploid | D | C | juice |
| sharp | Calville rouge d'hiver | late | 4 diploid | | C | |
| sharp | Calville blanc d'hiver | late | 4 triploid | D | C | juice |
| sharp | Vérité | late | 5 - 9 | | | |
| sharp | Court of Wick | mid | 3 self-sterile | D | | keeps well |
| sharp | Bramley's Seedling | mid to late | 2 triploid | | C | |
| sharp | Groseille | mid to late | 3 | | C | |
| sharp | Brown's Apple | mid to late | 4 diploid | | | |
| sweet | Eggleton Styre | early to mid | 4 - 6 | D | | |

| FLAVOUR TYPE | NAME | HARVEST SEASON | FLOWER GROUP | DES-SERT | CULI-NARY | OTHER USES |
|---|---|---|---|---|---|---|
| sweet | Fameuse | late | 3 | D | C | juice; keeps well |
| sweet | Pomeroy of Somerset | late | 4 | D | | |
| sweet | Sturmer Pippin | late | 4 | D | C | keeps well |
| sweet | Court Royal | late | 5 triploid | D | | |
| sweet | Rousse Latour | late (very) | 4 | | | |
| sweet | Fenouillet gris | mid | 2 | D | | |
| sweet | Antoinette | mid | 2 diploid | D | C | |
| sweet | Delaplace | mid | 3 | D | | |
| sweet | Gros Doux | mid | 4 -5 | D | | |
| sweet | Sweet Coppin | mid (late mid-season) | 4 | | | juice |
| sweet | Clozette | mid to late | 3 triploid | D | | |
| sweet | Belle cauchoise | mid-season | 3 - 4 diploid | D | C | |
| sweet | Yates | very late | 3 | D | C | |
| sweet | Roxbury Russett | very late | 2 - 3 | D | C | juice; keeps well |
| unknown | Red Normandy | unknown | 4 | | | |

# ENDNOTES

———⟡———

## \* SUMMER STIBBERT

From Bernwode Nurseries UK: 'The naming of several different apples, called Stubbard and Stibbert, has become very confused. They appear to be west country apples with a long history. Philip Miller in 1739 referred to a Stubbard's Apple as ripe in July, while others have described such apples as ripe in autumn.

Different ones are still known, but not the Stubbard we found in the Grove Heritage Collection in Tasmania, where many a 'lost' English apple found its way and a new home. They kindly sent scion wood.

We have observed its fruiting for a few years now and it seems most likely to be the old Michaelmas Stubbard. As the name suggests, the apples are ripe at the end of September (sometimes later) and are medium to large, with five obscure angles, russet at both ends and skin of pale green and streaks of dark red, broken with russet. It is a little sharp for dessert, but excellent as a cooker when it breaks down well but not all the way to a purée, though it would, if forced.

The flavour is fairly sharp and needs a little sugar but is very rich. In November and December they soften a little and are not so sharp.

The trees fruit when young and bear abundantly. The buds are brightly coloured with pink and red, and it has very large open flowers of rosy pink. Part tip bearing, but spurring well.'

## SYNONYMS FOR CALVILLE ROUGE D'HIVER:

Achte Rote Winter Calville, Achter Roter Winter Calvill, Achter Roter Winter Calville, Aechter Roter Winter Calvill, Aechter Roter Winter Calville, Aechter Rother Winter-Calvill, Blutroter Calvill, Blutroter Calville, Caillot Rosat, Caleville Musque, Caleville Sanguinole, Calleville Musque, Calleville Rouge, Calleville Rouge Couronnee, Calleville Rouge d'Hiver, Calleville Rouge de Paques, Calleville Royal d'Hiver, Calleville Sanguinole, Callot Rosat, Calvil Rosu de Iarna, Calvilla Rossa d'Hiver, Calvilla Rossa d'Inverno, Calvilla Rossa di Pasqua, Calville Acheter Rothe Winter, Calville d'Anjou, Calville d'Automne, Calville dit Sanguinole, Calville Flamense, Calville Imperiale, Calville Longue d'Hiver, Calville Musque, Calville Musque d'Hiver, Calville Musquee, Calville Passe Pomme d'Hiver, Calville Red, Calville Rosat, Calville Rouge, Calville Rouge Couronnee, Calville Rouge d'Anjou, Calville Rouge d'Anjou d'Hiver, Calville Rouge d'Automne, Calville Rouge d'Automne et d'Hiver, Calville Rouge de Normandie, Calville Rouge de Paques, Calville Rouge Dedans et Dehors, Calville rouge en dedans et en dehors, Calville Rouge Longue d'Hyver, Calville Rouge Normand, Calville Rouge Normande, Calville Rouge Sangue d'Hiver, Calville Royal d'Hiver, Calville

Royale d'Hiver, Calville Vrai des Allemands, Calville Vraie des Allemands, Cerveny Zimni Hranac, Coeur de Boeuf, Couchine, Cushman's Black, d'Outre-Passe, de Bretagne rouge, Echter Roter Winter Calvill, Gallwill Rusch, General, Gestreifter Muskat Calvill, Grosse Calville rouge d'hiver, Kalvil Krasnii Zimnii, Kalvil krasnyi zimnii, La Generale, Le General, Outre-Passe, Passe Pomme Cotelee, Passe Pomme Cotellee, Passe Pomme d'Automne, Passe Pomme d'Autumn, Passe Pomme d'Hiver, Passe-Pomme Cotelee, Passe-Pomme d'Automne, Passe-Pomme d'Hiver, Passe-Pomme Generale, Passe-Pomme Reouge Dedans, Passe-Pomme rouge en dedans et dehors, Passe-Pomme Soyette, Passe-Pomme Tardive, Pomme d'Outre Passe, Pomme D'Outre-Passe, Pomme de Bretagne Rouge, Pomme Outre Passe, Rambour Turc, Red Calville, Red Winter Calville, Red Winter-Calville, Rode Winter Calvill, Rode Winter Calville, Roode Paasch, Roode Winter Calville, Rote Winter Calville, Roter Eck Apfel, Roter Eckapfel, Roter Himbeer Apfel, Roter Oster Calvill, Roter Oster Kalvil, Roter Oster-Calvill, Roter Winter Calvill, Roter Winter Calville, Roter Winter Erdbeer Apfel, Roter Winter Erdbeerapfel, Roter Winter Himbeer Apfel, Roter Winter Himbeerapfel, Roter Winter Quitten Apfel, Roter Winter Quittenapfel, Roter Winterkalwil, Roter Winterquittenapfel, Rothe Winter Calville, Rother Winter-Calvill, Rouveau, Sanguinole, Teli piros kalvil, Vraie Calville Rouge d'Hiver, Winter Red Calville.[1]

---

1    *Calville Rouge D'Hiver. National Fruit Collection, UK*

## GRAVENSTEIN SYNONYMS:

Grafenstein, Almindelig Graasteensaeble, Blumen Calvill, Blumen Calville, Blumencalvill, Calville de Grafenstein, Calville de Gravenstein, Calville Grafensteiner, Calville Gravenstein, Calville Gravensteiner, Danish Graasteen, de Comte, de Gravenstein, de Princesse, der Graefensteiner, Diel's Sommerkonig, Diels Sommer Konig, Diels Sommerkonig, Early Congress, Ernteapfel, Gelber Gravensteiner, Graafen, Graasteen, Graasten, Graastensaeble, Graefenstein, Graefensteiner, Grafen Apfel, Grafen-Apfel, Grafenapfel, Grafenshteinskii kalvil, Grafenshteinskoe zbeltoe, Grafenstain, Grafensteiner, Grafensteinskoe, Grafszt ynek, Grafsztynek Prawdziwy, Graistynek, Grave Slige, Grave Slije, Grave Sliji, Grave Stige, Grave Stigne, Grave Stije, Gravensteen, Gravensteener, Gravenstein Apple, Gravensteiner, Gravensteiner (Gul), Gravensteini alma, Gravensteinsapple, Gravenstener, Gravenstine, Gravstynke, GravstynskT, Greastener, Gul Graastener, Gult Graasteensaeble, Harryman, Ohio Nonpareil, Pansky vonac, Paradies, Paradies Apfel, Paradiesapfel, Petergaard, Petersgaards Graasten, Pomme de Gravenstein, Pomme Graefenstein, Prinzessin Apfel, Prinzessinapfel, Ripp Apfel, Rippapfel, Romarin de Botzen, Sabin, Sabine, Sabine (des Flamands), Sabine (of the Flemings), Sabine of the Flemings, Savine, Sommer Koning, Sommerkonig, Stroemling, Strohmer, Stromerling, Stromling, The Gravenstein Apple, Tom Harryman.[2]

---

2     *Gravenstein. National Fruit Collection, UK*

## King of the Pippins synonyms

Aranyparmen, die Englische Winter-Goldparmane, Englische Winter Gold Parmaene, Englische Winter Gold Parmane, Englische Winter Gold Pearmain, Englische Winter Gold-Parmane, Englische Winter Golden Pearmain, Englische Winter Goldparmane, Englische Winter Winter-Gold-Parmane, Englische Winter-Gold-Parmane, Englische Winter-Goldparmane, Englische Wintergoldparmane, English Winter Golden Pear, George I, George II, Gold Parmaene, Gold Parmane, Golden Winter Pearmain, Golden Winter-Pearmain, Golden-Winter-Pearmain, Goldparmane, Goldreinette, Guld Pearmain, Guld-Pearmain, Guldparman, Guldpearmain, Gullparman, Hampshire Golden Pippin, Hampshire King of the Pippins, Hampshire Yellow, Hampshire Yellow Golden Pippin, Hamshire Yellow, Herzogs Reinette, Jone's Southampton Pippin, Jones, Jones Southampton Pippin, Jones Southampton Pippins, Jones' Southampton Pippin, Jones' Southampton Yellow, Jones's Southampton Pippin, King of Pippins, King of the Pippin, King Pippin, Krolowa renet, Orange Pearmain, Parm einette, Parmain d'Or, Parmain Doree, Parmaine Doree, Parmen zimnii zolotoi, Parmena zlata, Parmena zlata zimna, Parmena zlata zimni, Pearmain Dorata, Pearmain Dorato, Pearmain dorato d'inverno, Pearmain Dore, Pearmain Dore d'hiver, Pearmain Doree, Pearmain Doree d'Hiver, Pearmain-doree d'hiver, Pike's Pearmain, Polosatii Safran, Polosatii shafran, Prince of Pippins, Prince's Pippin, Princess Pippin, Queen of the Pippins, Regina delle Renette, Reine des Reinettes, Reinette d'Oree, Reinette de Friesland Hative, Reinette de la Couronne, Reinette

Siavee, Seek no Farther, Seek no Further, Seek-no-Further, Shropshire Pippin, Teli arany parmen, The King of Pippins, Ventinus Ellacott, Ventinuss Ellicott Pippin, Ventmus Ellicott Pippin, Ventmuss Ellicot, Ventmuss Ellicott, Ventmuss Ellicott Pippin, Vermillon Raye, Vermillon Rayee, Vinter Guldpearmain, Winter Gol Parmane, Winter Gold Parmaene, Winter Gold Parmane, Winter Gold Pearmain, Winter Goldparmane, Winter Pearmain, Winter-Gold-Parmane, Winter-Goldparmane, Wintergoldparmane, Zimni zlote parmena, Zimnii zolotoi parmen, Zlata zimni parmena, Zlatna parmena, Zlota Reneta, Zlotoi Parmen.[3]

---

3     *King of the Pippins. National Fruit Collection, UK*

# BIBLIOGRAPHY

─────────⟨○⟩─────────

Bailey, Liberty Hyde. *Cyclopedia of American Horticulture*. Wilhelm Miller Edition: 2, 1902.

Beach, Spencer Ambrose; Booth, Nathaniel Ogden and Taylor, Orin Morehouse. *The Apples of New York*. New York (State). Dept. of Agriculture, New York State Agricultural Experiment Station, 1905.

Bellman, R. B.; Gallander, J. F. *Wine Deacidification*. In Chichester, C. O.; Mrak, Emil Marcel; Stewart, George Franklin. Advances in Food Research Vol. 25. Academic Press, 1979.

Bore, J.M. and Fleckinger, J. *Pommiers a Cidre*. Quae, 1997.

Hedrick, U.P. and Henry, George. *Apples: Old and New*. New York Agricultural Experiment Station, 1913

Herefordshire County Council. *Bulmer's Cider— How It All Began*. Herefordshire Through Time. 2012.

Hogg, Robert and Bull, Henry Graves. *The Herefordshire Pomona*. Herefordshire, UK. The Pomona Committee of the Woolhope Naturalists' Field Club of Hereford, 1884.

Hogg, Robert. *The Fruit Manual*. London, Journal of Horticulture Office, 1884.

Hogg, Robert. *The Apple & Pear as Vintage Fruits.* Hereford. Jakeman & Carver, 1886

Howat, Jez and Lea, Andrew. *Styling Cider.* Cider Workshop, UK

Jolicoeur, Claude. *The New Cider Maker's Handbook.* Vermont, USA. Chelsea Green Publishing 2013

Martell, Charles. *Native Apples of Gloucestershire.* Gloucestershire Orchard Group (ongoing)

Ministère de l'agriculture. *Variétés recommandées de pommiers à cidre, pour les départements de Normandie, de Bretagne, et du Maine et Perche.* Normandy, France, 2007.

Morgan, J. & Richards, A. (Illus. Dowle, E.) *The New Book of Apples.* Ebury Press; Revised edition (February 19, 2003)

Pickering, David. *Growing Cider Apples.* Orange, NSW, Australia. NSW Dept. of Primary Industries, 2008

Winmill, Clive. *Apples Old and New*, Edition 5. Victoria, Australia. Badger's Keep, 1997.

# Index

# Some Heritage Fruit Groups in Australia

**Werribee Park Heritage Orchard,** situated near Melbourne, Victoria (Australia) is a beautiful antique orchard dating from the 1870s, on the grounds of the old mansion by the Werribee River. It was renowned for its peaches, grapes, apples, quinces, pears, a variety of plums and several other fruits, as well as walnuts and olives. Over the past few decades the orchard was forgotten and—through neglect—fell into ruin. Recently this historic treasure has been rediscovered. Volunteers are replanting and tending the orchard.

**The Heritage Fruits Society** is based in Melbourne, Australia. Their aim is to conserve heritage fruit varieties on private and public land. They enable and encourage society members to research this wide range of varieties and to inform the public on the benefits of heritage fruits for health, sustainability and biodiversity.

Petty's Orchard in Templestowe, Victoria, Australia, is one of Melbourne's oldest commercial orchards, and it holds the largest collection of heritage/heirloom apple varieties on mainland Australia, with more than two hundred varieties of old and rare apples. The maintenance of the apple tree collection is done by Heritage Fruits Society volunteers.

**The Rare Fruit Society of South Australia** is an amateur organisation of fruit tree growers who preserve heritage varieties, explore climate limitations and study propagation, pruning and grafting techniques.

Printed in Great Britain
by Amazon

84955777R10080